From Novice to Novelist
Quick Tips for Budding Writers

Michael Scott Bertrand

Table of Contents

A Note from the Author

Let me tell you what this book is not.

This is not a workbook. It is not a step-by-step guide. It is not some activity book filled with useless prompts and silly exercises.

This is a book of simple tips that can help you write better fiction. If you're a beginner, this book can help you with the basics of turning words into sentences, sentences into paragraphs and paragraphs into a complete story. If you're a more seasoned writer, perhaps you'll find some old lessons that you had forgotten.

The chapters are short. They are short because, in my humble opinion, you should just read one or two and then get back to writing. That is, after all, what you're trying to master.

So if your characters feel like cardboard cutouts, and your plot twists fall flat, this book has got you covered. We'll discuss the basic tools you need as writer—as well as some more advanced tricks—and put you on the path to becoming a successful and productive author.

Every author has taken a different path to get where they are. I spent many years in government and politics. In those fields I crafted countless speeches, issue briefings and press releases. Later—after I had decided to pursue my passion for writing full-time, writing novels and shorts stories—I found those "old" skills served me well. I had developed my own style: conversational, somewhat friendly, occasionally witty.

Whatever path you took to get here today, celebrate it! Your backstory—past jobs, past loves, past adventures—will help you as you forge ahead as an author. Recognizing your uniqueness will help you find what every author seeks: an honest, authentic voice.

Happy writing, and I hope you find the tips in this book useful.

MSB

Try to Write Every Day

Writing is one of the most fulfilling and rewarding experiences one can have in life. It's a way to express oneself, to explore the world, and to communicate with others. However, writing can also be challenging, intimidating, and overwhelming. That's why many people find themselves struggling to write consistently, or even to start writing at all. They might be intimidated by the blank page, unsure of their abilities, or simply too busy with other things in their lives.

But the truth is, writing is a skill that can be developed with practice, just like any other skill. And one of the best ways to improve your writing is to write every day, even if it's just a few sentences.

Now, you might be thinking, "Every day? That sounds like a lot of work!" But hear me out. Writing every day doesn't have to be a chore. It can be a fun and enjoyable experience, a way to connect with yourself and your thoughts, and a way to develop your writing skills over time.

Here are some reasons why writing every day is so beneficial:

✓ ***First of all, writing every day helps you develop a writing habit.*** When you make writing a part of your daily routine, it becomes easier and more natural over time. You start to look forward to your writing time, rather than dreading it or putting it off.

✓ ***Secondly, writing every day helps you stay connected with your creative side.*** When you write consistently, you keep the creative juices flowing, and you're more likely to come up with new ideas and insights. Even if you're just writing a few sentences a day, you're still engaging your brain in the act of creation, and that's always a good thing.

✓ ***Thirdly, writing every day helps you build your writing skills.*** The more you write, the better you get at it. You start to develop a sense of what works and what doesn't, what your strengths are and where you need to improve. And even if you're not working on a specific project, writing every day helps you hone your writing voice and style, so that when you do sit down to write something more substantial, you're already in the groove.

✓ ***Finally, writing every day helps you stay motivated and accountable.*** When you commit to writing every day, you're making a promise to yourself. You're saying, "This is important to me, and I'm going to make time for it." And when you see yourself making progress, even if it's just a little bit each day, you feel good about yourself and your abilities.

So how do you start writing every day, even if it's just a few sentences?

> ‣ Set aside a specific time each day for writing, whether it's first thing in the morning, during your lunch break, or before you go to bed.
>
> ‣ Find a comfortable and inspiring writing space, whether it's a quiet corner of your home or a cozy café.
>
> ‣ Use prompts or writing exercises to get started if you're not sure what to write about.
>
> ‣ Keep a journal or notebook with you at all times, so you can jot down ideas whenever they come to you.
>
> ‣ Celebrate your successes, no matter how small they may seem. Every sentence you write is a step forward in your writing journey.

Writing every day, even if it's just a few sentences, is one of the best things you can do for your writing practice. It helps you develop a writing habit, stay connected with your creativity, build your writing skills, and stay motivated and accountable. So don't be afraid to start small and make writing a part of your daily routine.

Read Wisely and Consistently

When it comes to becoming a better writer, there is no shortcut or magic formula that will instantly transform you into the next Toni Morrison, Ernest Hemingway or James Patterson. However, there is one piece of advice that all successful writers will agree on: read wisely and consistently. This is the foundation upon which all other writing skills are built, and it is something that you can start doing today, no matter where you are on your writing journey.

So, what does it mean to read wisely and consistently? It means that you should read widely, exploring different genres and styles of writing, and that you should read regularly, making it a part of your daily routine. The benefits of doing so are numerous and far-reaching, and they will help you become a better writer in ways that you might not even realize.

First and foremost, reading widely exposes you to different ways of thinking and writing. It expands your knowledge and worldview, and it helps you understand the complexities of the human experience. By reading different genres, you'll learn how to craft compelling characters, build suspenseful plots, and create vivid descriptions. You'll also gain insight into the various writing techniques and styles used by different authors, which you can then adapt to your own writing.

Reading consistently helps you develop your own writing voice. As you read more and more, you'll start to identify the writers who inspire you and resonate with you. You'll start to see patterns in their writing that you can then incorporate into your own work. This doesn't mean that you should copy their writing style, but rather that you should learn from them and use their work as a source of inspiration.

Reading widely and consistently also helps you develop a strong vocabulary and an understanding of grammar and sentence structure. This is because reading exposes you to different types of writing, which in turn exposes you to different words, phrases, and sentence structures. You'll start to pick up on common writing patterns and techniques, and you'll be able to apply them to your own writing.

But reading isn't just about improving your writing skills. It also has numerous other benefits that can improve your overall quality of life. For one, it helps reduce stress and anxiety. Reading has been shown to be an effective stress-reliever, helping people to relax and unwind after a long day. It can also improve your memory and cognitive function, keeping your brain sharp and active as you age.

So, how can you start reading wisely and consistently? First, make it a priority in your daily routine. Set aside a specific time each day to read, whether it's before bed, during your lunch break, or in the morning with your coffee. Make it a habit, and stick to it, even if it's just for a few minutes each day.

Next, choose books that interest you and that challenge you. Don't be afraid to step outside your comfort zone and explore different genres and styles of writing. Read classics, contemporary fiction, non-fiction, poetry, and anything else that catches your eye. The more you read, the more you'll learn, and the more you'll be able to incorporate into your own writing.

Finally, join a book club or writing group. This will give you the opportunity to discuss the books you're reading with other like-minded individuals, and to get feedback on your own writing. It's also a great way to stay motivated and to hold yourself accountable for your reading and writing goals.

Reading wisely and consistently is an essential part of becoming a better writer. It expands your knowledge, improves your writing skills, and has numerous other benefits that can improve your overall quality of life. So, pick up a book today—maybe an old favorite—and start reading!

Use Prompts for Inspiration

Writing can be a deeply rewarding experience, but sometimes finding inspiration can be a challenge. One way to overcome writer's block and get your creative juices flowing is by using prompts. Prompts are short phrases or sentences that give you a starting point for your writing. They can be anything from a simple word or phrase to a more complex scenario or character description. By using prompts, you can explore new ideas and perspectives, push your boundaries, and develop your writing skills.

Prompts are a great way to get started on a new writing project. They can help you overcome the blank page syndrome that often plagues writers. When you're staring at a blank page, it can be difficult to know where to start. By using a prompt, you have a starting point that can help you get your thoughts and ideas down on paper. This can be especially helpful if you're working on a longer piece of writing like a novel or screenplay.

One of the benefits of using prompts is that they can help you explore new ideas and perspectives. Sometimes we get stuck in a rut with our writing, repeating the same themes or characters over and over again. By using prompts, you can challenge yourself to think outside the box and try something new. For example, if you typically write romance stories, a prompt that challenges you to write a horror story can help you flex your creative muscles and explore new genres.

Writing prompts can challenge you to write in different styles, tones, and genres, helping you to become a more versatile and adaptable writer. For example, a prompt that challenges you to write in the style of a certain author can help you learn to emulate their voice and writing style. A prompt that challenges you to write a story from multiple perspectives can help you develop your skills at writing from different points of view.

Prompts can also be a fun way to get your creative juices flowing. They can challenge you to think creatively and come up with new and exciting ideas. Writing can be a solitary experience, but prompts can make it more fun and engaging. For example, a prompt that challenges you to write a story about a talking animal can be a fun and lighthearted way to get started on a new project.

If you're not sure where to find prompts, there are countless resources available. There are books and websites dedicated to writing prompts, as well as apps that generate prompts at random. You can also create your own prompts by thinking about your interests, experiences, and the themes you want to explore in your writing.

When using prompts, it's important to remember that they are just a starting point. They are meant to inspire you and get you thinking creatively, but you don't have to follow them exactly. Use them as a jumping-off point, but don't be afraid to take your writing in a different direction if that's where your creativity takes you. The goal is to get your creative juices flowing and develop your writing skills, not to follow a set of rigid guidelines.

Prompts can be a valuable tool for writers of all skill levels. They can help you overcome writer's block, explore new ideas and perspectives, develop your writing skills, and have fun with your writing. Whether you're a seasoned writer or just starting out, using prompts can help you become a better and more creative writer.

Write First, Edit Later

As a writer, it's easy to get bogged down in the details of your work. You might find yourself obsessing over word choice, sentence structure, and punctuation, all before you've even finished your first draft. While editing is an important part of the writing process, it's important not to let it distract you from your primary goal: writing. That's why one of the most valuable pieces of advice you can receive as a writer is to "write first, edit later."

When you sit down to write, your focus should be on getting your ideas down on paper. Don't worry about making everything perfect - that can come later. Just let your ideas flow and see where they take you. This is sometimes called "free writing" or "stream of consciousness" writing. The goal is to get your thoughts down on paper without worrying about how they sound or whether they're grammatically correct.

Writing first and editing later has a number of benefits. For one thing, it allows you to get into a flow state. When you're not worried about editing as you write, you can get into a rhythm and focus solely on your ideas. This can lead to more creative and insightful writing, as you're not getting bogged down in the technical details.

Writing first and editing later can also help you overcome writer's block. Often, writer's block is caused by a fear of not being perfect. If you're constantly editing as you write, you're putting extra pressure on yourself to get everything right the first time. This can be paralyzing, and can prevent you from making progress on your work. By allowing yourself to write freely, without worrying about perfection, you can get over that initial hump and start making progress.

Another benefit of this approach is that it can help you see your work with fresh eyes. When you finish your first draft and come back to it later for editing, you'll have a better sense of what's working and what's not. You'll also be able to see your work from a more objective perspective, as you'll have some distance from it. This can help you make more effective edits and revisions.

Of course, editing is an important part of the writing process. Once you've finished your first draft, it's time to go back and make edits. This is where you can fine-tune your work and make sure it's as polished as possible. But by separating the writing and editing processes, you're allowing yourself to be more effective at each step. You're not trying to do everything at once, which can lead to overwhelm and burnout.

Writing first and editing later is a valuable approach for writers of all skill levels. By allowing yourself to write freely, without worrying about perfection, you can tap into your creativity and overcome writer's block. And by separating the writing and editing processes, you can be more effective at each step.

It's OK to Make Mistakes

It's natural to want your work to be perfect. You want every sentence to be flawless, every idea to be brilliant, and every piece to be a masterpiece. But the reality is that writing is a process, and it's impossible to get everything right on the first try. That's why it's important not to be afraid to make mistakes as a writer.

Making mistakes is a natural part of the learning process. As a writer, you're constantly learning and growing, and mistakes are a necessary part of that growth. Every time you make a mistake, you're learning something new. Maybe you'll discover a new technique that works better for you, or maybe you'll learn to avoid a common pitfall. Either way, mistakes can be valuable learning experiences.

Another reason not to be afraid of making mistakes is that they can lead to breakthroughs. Sometimes, the most interesting and innovative ideas come from mistakes. When you're not afraid to take risks and try new things, you open yourself up to new possibilities. You might stumble upon a new approach or idea that you never would have considered otherwise.

But perhaps the most important reason not to be afraid of making mistakes is that it can hold you back as a writer. If you're constantly worried about making mistakes, you might be hesitant to try new things or take risks. This can lead to stagnation and a lack of growth. It's important to remember that mistakes are a necessary part of the creative process, and that you can't grow as a writer without making them.

Of course, this doesn't mean that you should embrace mistakes for their own sake. It's still important to strive for excellence in your writing. But it's also important to remember that perfection is an unattainable goal. No matter how good you get, there will always be room for improvement. By embracing mistakes and using them as opportunities to learn and grow, you can become a better writer over time.

So how can you embrace mistakes as a writer? Here are a few tips:

> **Be willing to take risks:** Don't be afraid to try something new or take a different approach to your writing.

> **Learn from your mistakes:** When you do make a mistake, take the time to reflect on what went wrong and how you can avoid it in the future.

> **Don't beat yourself up:** Making mistakes is natural. Don't let it get you down or discourage you from continuing to write.

> **Keep writing:** The best way to improve as a writer is to keep writing. The more you write, the more comfortable you'll become with the process, and the more mistakes you'll make. And that's okay!

Don't be afraid to make mistakes as a writer. Embrace them as opportunities to learn and grow, and don't let the fear of making mistakes hold you back. Remember that writing is a process, and that mistakes are a natural part of that process. Keep writing, keep learning, and keep improving.

Experiment with Different Styles

As a writer, it's easy to get stuck in a rut. You might find yourself writing the same type of content over and over again, using the same writing style and format. While this can be comfortable, it can also be limiting. Experimenting with different writing styles and formats can help you grow as a writer and expand your creative horizons.

Here are just a few examples:

- **Fiction:** That's what this book is about! Whether you prefer short stories or novels, writing fiction can be a rewarding experience. It allows you to create your own worlds and characters, and to explore themes and ideas in a way that's different from nonfiction writing.

- **Poetry:** If you've never tried writing poetry before, give it a shot. It can be a great way to explore your emotions and express yourself in a different way.

- **Creative nonfiction:** This genre combines the storytelling of fiction with the factual accuracy of journalism. It can be a great way to explore real-world issues and events in a way that's engaging and thought-provoking.

▸ *__Blogging:__* If you haven't tried blogging before, you should consider it. It can be a great way to build your online presence and connect with readers on a more personal level. Many websites provide low or no-cost ways to introduce yourself to the blogging world.

▸ *__Screenwriting:__* If you're interested in film or television, trying your hand at screenwriting can be a lot of fun. It allows you to tell stories visually, and to explore the intricacies of character and plot in a way that's unique to the screen.

The possibilities are endless. Experimenting with different writing styles and formats can help you discover new strengths and weaknesses, and can help you grow as a writer.

A few tips to get you started:

✓**Start small:** Don't feel like you need to jump right into a novel or a feature-length screenplay. Start with something small, like a short story or a blog post.

✓**Do your research:** Before you start writing in a new style or format, take the time to research it. Read examples from other writers, and learn the conventions and best practices of the genre.

✓**Be patient:** Experimenting with new writing styles and formats can be challenging. Don't get discouraged if it takes you a while to get the hang of it.

✓**Get feedback:** Share your work with others and ask for feedback. This can help you identify areas where you need to improve, and can give you the encouragement you need to keep going.

Experimenting with different writing styles and formats can be a fun and rewarding experience. It allows you to grow as a writer and explore new creative horizons. Don't be afraid to try something new, and remember to be patient and persistent. With time and practice, you can become a master of multiple writing styles and formats.

Keep a Journal of Ideas

As a writer, it's essential to capture ideas as they come to you, and one of the best ways to do that is to keep a notebook or journal. Whether you're writing fiction, non-fiction, or even just journaling for personal growth, having a place to jot down ideas can be incredibly beneficial.

One of the most significant benefits of keeping a notebook or journal is that it allows you to capture ideas as they come to you. Writing down your ideas, no matter how small or insignificant they may seem at the time, can help you develop them into something more substantial later on. You never know when a small idea could turn into a fully-fledged story or article.

Additionally, a notebook or journal is an excellent tool for brainstorming. When you're stuck on a particular idea or plot point, jotting down your thoughts can help you work through it. It can also be a helpful way to organize your ideas and create an outline for your work.

Keeping a notebook or journal also allows you to look back on your writing journey and see how far you've come. It can be incredibly motivating to see how much progress you've made, especially when you're feeling stuck or discouraged.

Here are a few tips for keeping a successful writing notebook or journal:

- **Keep it with you at all times:** You never know when inspiration will strike, so make sure you always have your notebook or journal with you. Whether you prefer a physical notebook or a digital one on your phone, make it easily accessible.

- **Write down everything:** Don't filter or judge your ideas as they come to you. Write down anything and everything that comes to mind, even if it seems silly or unimportant. You can always edit and refine later.

- **Use it for more than just writing:** Your notebook or journal doesn't have to be limited to just writing ideas. You can use it to keep track of quotes, to-do lists, goals, and even personal reflections.

- **Set aside time for journaling:** While it's essential to capture ideas as they come to you, it's also important to set aside time for dedicated journaling. This can be a helpful way to reflect on your writing journey and process.

- **Review and revise:** Don't let your notebook or journal become a graveyard for ideas. Periodically review your entries and revise or develop them further.

Keeping a notebook—or mastering the notes app on your phone—is an essential tool for any writer. It allows you to capture ideas as they come to you, brainstorm, organize your thoughts, and track your progress. Don't let those good ideas slip away into the ether!

Write What You Know

"Write what you know" is a common piece of advice that writers often hear. But what does it really mean, and how can you apply it to your own writing?

At its core, "write what you know" means drawing from your own experiences and knowledge to create compelling, authentic stories. It doesn't necessarily mean you have to write only about your personal experiences, but rather to use them as inspiration for your work.

One of the biggest advantages of writing what you know is that it allows you to infuse your writing with authenticity and depth. When you draw on your own experiences and emotions, you can create characters and situations that feel real and relatable.

Writing what you know also allows you to explore themes and topics that you're passionate about. By writing about something that resonates with you on a personal level, you're more likely to create work that's meaningful and engaging.

Things to keep in mind when applying this advice:

- ▸ ***Expand your definition of "what you know":*** Writing what you know doesn't have to be limited to your personal experiences. You can also draw from your professional expertise, research, and the experiences of people around you. For example, if you're not a doctor but you're passionate about medical issues, you can research and interview doctors to gain a deeper understanding of the subject.

- ▸ ***Avoid using real-life people or events:*** While drawing from your own experiences can be a powerful tool in writing, it's important to remember that using real-life people or events in your work can be problematic. Not only can it lead to legal issues, but it can also hurt your relationships with the people involved. Instead, use your experiences as inspiration, but allow your imagination to take over.

- ▸ ***Don't be afraid to take creative liberties:*** Just because you're writing what you know doesn't mean you have to stick strictly to the facts. Creative liberties can make your work more engaging and exciting. However, be mindful of how far you stray from the truth, and make sure your changes are serving the story, rather than just for the sake of adding drama.

- ▸ ***Use your own voice:*** When writing what you know, it's important to use your own voice and style. Don't try to emulate other writers or adopt a style that doesn't feel natural to you. Your unique perspective and voice are what make your work stand out.

Writing what you know can be a powerful tool for creating compelling, authentic stories. By drawing on your own experiences, expertise, and passions, you can create work that's meaningful, engaging, and relatable.

Write What You're Passionate About

When it comes to writing, there is no one-size-fits-all approach. However, one of the most important pieces of advice any writer can receive is to write what they're passionate about. Writing about topics that truly interest and inspire you is the key to creating work that is authentic, engaging, and fulfilling.

Writing about what you're passionate about not only makes the writing process more enjoyable, but it can also lead to better writing. When you're passionate about a topic, you're more likely to put in the time and effort necessary to research and craft your work. This can result in a higher quality piece of writing that resonates with your audience.

Passionate writing can also help you connect with your readers on a deeper level. If you're writing about a topic that you're genuinely interested in, chances are that your enthusiasm will shine through in your writing. This can create a stronger emotional connection between you and your readers, helping to keep them engaged and interested in your work.

Here are some tips for writing about what you're passionate about:

▸ **Identify your passions:** Take some time to think about what you're truly passionate about. What topics do you find yourself thinking about or talking about frequently? What do you enjoy learning about or researching in your spare time? Make a list of these topics and consider how you could incorporate them into your writing.

▸ **Don't limit yourself:** Your passions don't have to be limited to one particular topic or genre. You may find that you're passionate about a variety of subjects, and that's okay! Embrace your interests and use them to inspire your writing.

▸ **Explore your passions:** Once you've identified your passions, take the time to explore them further. Read books, watch documentaries, attend events or conferences, and engage with others who share your interests. This can help you deepen your knowledge and understanding of your passions, making it easier to write about them in a compelling way.

▸ **Be authentic:** When you're writing about what you're passionate about, it's important to be true to yourself. Don't try to write about something just because you think it will be popular or successful. Write about what you truly care about, and your authenticity will shine through in your writing.

▸ **Use your passion to inspire others:** Writing about what you're passionate about can also be a powerful way to inspire others. When you share your enthusiasm for a particular topic, it can motivate and inspire others to learn more and get involved.

Writing what you're passionate about is a powerful way to create work that is authentic, engaging, and fulfilling. By identifying your passions—and using those passions to inspire others—you can create writing that truly resonates with your readers.

Take Writing Workshops or Classes

Writing is a craft that takes practice and dedication to perfect. While you can certainly learn a lot on your own, taking writing workshops or classes can be a great way to improve your skills and take your writing to the next level. Here's why they can beneficial:

✓*Learn from experts:* Writing workshops and classes are often taught by experienced writers who can offer valuable insights and feedback on your work. They can help you identify your strengths and weaknesses, and give you guidance on how to improve.

✓*Get feedback:* One of the biggest benefits of taking a writing workshop or class is the opportunity to get feedback on your work. You'll be able to share your writing with others and receive constructive criticism that can help you grow as a writer.

✓*Meet other writers:* Writing can be a solitary pursuit, but taking a writing workshop or class can help you connect with other writers who share your passion. You'll be able to share ideas, offer support, and build a community of like-minded individuals.

✓*Stay motivated:* Writing can be challenging, and it's easy to get discouraged when you hit a rough patch. Taking a writing workshop or class can help you stay motivated and inspired. You'll be able to set goals, receive feedback, and stay accountable to your writing practice.

✓*Try new things:* Writing workshops and classes often offer the opportunity to try new things and experiment with different writing styles and genres. You might discover a new passion or talent that you didn't know you had.

If you're interested in taking a writing workshop or class, there are a few things to keep in mind:

▸**Research your options:** There are a lot of different writing workshops and classes out there, so it's important to do your research and find one that suits your needs and interests. Your local community college might be a good place to start.

▸**Set goals:** Before you start your workshop or class, set some goals for what you want to achieve. This will help you stay focused and motivated throughout the experience.

▸**Be open to feedback:** Remember that feedback is an essential part of the writing process, and be open to constructive criticism from your instructor and peers.

▸**Participate actively:** To get the most out of your workshop or class, be an active participant. Engage in discussions, ask questions, and offer feedback to others.

▸**Practice, practice, practice:** Finally, remember that the key to improving your writing skills is practice. Take what you learn in your workshop or class and apply it to your writing practice outside of class.

Taking a writing workshop or class can be a great way to improve your skills, connect with other writers, and stay motivated. With the right mindset and approach, you can get the most out of your experience and take your writing to the next level.

Be Open to Feedback and Criticism

As a writer, one of the most valuable things you can do is be open to feedback and criticism. While it can be difficult to hear negative feedback on something you've poured your heart and soul into, it's important to remember that feedback is an essential part of the writing process.

Remember, authors want people to read what they've written! So while it may hurt to hear that your writing needs some work, it's better to hear that from a beta reader than from a one-star review.

Being open to feedback and criticism can help you become a better writer:

✓ ***Gain a new perspective:*** When you're working on a piece of writing, it's easy to get tunnel vision and lose sight of the bigger picture. Feedback and criticism from others can help you see your work from a new perspective and identify areas that need improvement.

✓ ***Identify strengths and weaknesses:*** Feedback can help you identify your strengths as a writer, as well as areas where you need to improve. This can be incredibly helpful when it comes to honing your craft and becoming a more well-rounded writer.

✓*Improve your writing:* Constructive criticism can be tough to hear, but it can also be incredibly helpful in improving your writing. If someone points out a flaw in your writing, use that feedback to make your work better.

✓*Learn from others:* Everyone has different experiences and perspectives, and feedback from others can help you learn from their experiences and expand your own knowledge base.

✓*Build resilience*: Writing can be a tough business, and rejection and criticism are inevitable. Learning to handle feedback and criticism gracefully can help you build resilience and develop a thick skin, which can be incredibly helpful in navigating the ups and downs of the writing life.

If you're struggling with receiving feedback and criticism, approach it with an open mind:

▸ **Remember that feedback is not a reflection of your worth as a person or a writer.** It's simply an opportunity to learn and grow.

▸ **Try to separate your emotions from your work**. This can be difficult, but it's important to approach feedback with an open mind and a willingness to learn.

▸ **Ask questions.** If you're not sure why someone is giving you a particular piece of feedback, ask for clarification. This can help you understand their perspective and use the feedback more effectively.

▸**Take time to process feedback.** If you're feeling overwhelmed or emotional after receiving feedback, take some time to step back and process your feelings before taking action.

▸**Look for patterns.** If you receive similar feedback from multiple sources, pay attention to it. This can be a sign that there's something you need to work on in your writing.

Being open to feedback and criticism can be a powerful tool in becoming a better writer. Remember to be kind to yourself and to others, and to use feedback as a tool for growth and improvement.

To Outline or Not to Outline

Are you the type of writer who likes to dive headfirst into a story, letting the characters and plot develop naturally as you go along? Or do you prefer to plan out every detail ahead of time, crafting a detailed outline before you even put pen to paper? The debate over outlining versus "pantsing" (writing by the seat of your pants) is a long-standing one in the writing world, and there are pros and cons to both approaches.

Let's start with outlining. Many writers swear by the power of a good outline, and there are certainly advantages to this approach. Outlining allows you to plan out your story in advance, making it easier to see the big picture and ensure that all the pieces fit together. It can also help you avoid writer's block by giving you a clear roadmap to follow.

There are many different ways to create an outline. Some writers—James Patterson, for one—prefer to use a detailed, chapter-by-chapter outline, while others prefer a looser, more general outline that simply lists the major plot points. Still, others use a combination of both, creating a general outline first and then adding more detail as they go along.

One potential drawback of outlining is that it can feel constraining to some writers. If you've planned out every detail of your story in advance, you may feel like you don't have the freedom to explore new ideas or let your characters take the story in unexpected directions. Outlining can also be time-consuming, and some writers find that it takes the joy out of the writing process.

On the other hand, "pantsing" can be a liberating approach for some writers. When you write by the seat of your pants, you have the freedom to let your story evolve naturally, following your characters wherever they may lead. This approach can be especially effective for writers who thrive on spontaneity and creative energy. Stephen King is probably the most well-known pantser in today's literary world.

There are potential downsides to pantsing. Without a clear plan or roadmap, it can be easy to get lost or lose track of your story's direction. You may find yourself hitting a wall or struggling to come up with ideas as you go along. Additionally, if you're writing a complex plot with multiple characters and storylines, pantsing can make it difficult to keep everything straight and ensure that all the pieces fit together.

Ultimately, the decision to outline or not to outline comes down to personal preference. There's no right or wrong way to approach writing, and what works for one writer may not work for another. Some writers prefer to create a loose outline or framework, giving them a sense of direction without constraining their creativity too much. Others may prefer to dive right in and let the story take shape as they write.

Regardless of which approach you choose, it's important to remember that writing is a process, and there will always be ups and downs along the way. Whether you're a pantser or a plotter, the most important thing is to keep writing and keep honing your craft. With practice and perseverance, you can find the approach that works best for you and develop your own unique voice as a writer.

Should You Write a Novel or Short Stories?

Are you torn between writing a novel or short stories? As a writer, it can be difficult to decide which form of storytelling is right for you. Both have their advantages and disadvantages, and ultimately, the decision depends on your writing goals and preferences. So, let's explore the differences between writing a novel and short stories to help you make an informed decision.

First, let's start with the basics. A novel is a long-form work of fiction that typically ranges between 80,000 and 100,000 words or more. It tells a complex, multi-layered story with multiple characters, subplots, and themes. On the other hand, a short story is a brief work of fiction that typically ranges between 1,000 and 10,000 words. It tells a focused, self-contained story with a limited number of characters and a singular theme.

Advantages of writing a novel:

✓Room for depth and complexity: A novel allows you to explore your characters, themes, and plot in greater depth than a short story. You have more space to develop your ideas and create a fully-realized world.

✓Opportunity for series: Writing a novel gives you the opportunity to create a series of books that follow the same characters and world, allowing you to build a loyal fanbase.

✓Potential for bigger payoff: A well-written novel can bring greater commercial success and critical acclaim than a short story.

Disadvantages of writing a novel:

▸ Time-consuming: Writing a novel is a long and often arduous process that can take months or even years to complete.

▸ Risk of losing focus: With so much material to work with, it can be easy to lose focus and become overwhelmed.

▸ Difficulty in revision: Revising a novel can be a daunting task, requiring you to keep track of multiple plotlines, characters, and themes.

Advantages of writing short stories:

✓Opportunity for experimentation: Short stories give you the opportunity to experiment with different styles, genres, and themes without committing to a full-length novel.

✓Faster turnaround time: Short stories can be written and revised more quickly than a novel, allowing you to produce more work in a shorter amount of time.

✓Greater likelihood of publication: Short stories are often easier to place in literary magazines and anthologies, providing opportunities for publication and exposure.

Disadvantages of writing short stories:

▸ Limited scope: Due to their brevity, short stories have a limited scope, and it can be challenging to fully develop characters, plotlines, and themes.

▸ Less commercial potential: While short stories can bring critical acclaim and recognition, they typically don't offer the same commercial potential as a novel.

▸ Difficulty in building a fanbase: Short stories are often seen as a more niche form of storytelling, and it can be challenging to build a loyal fanbase.

So, should you write a novel or short stories? Ultimately, the answer depends on your personal writing goals and preferences. If you're interested in exploring complex characters, themes, and plotlines, and you're willing to commit to a longer writing process, then a novel may be the right choice for you. However, if you're interested in experimenting with different styles, genres, and themes, and you want to produce work more quickly, then short stories may be a better fit.

Crafting a Compelling Plotline

Crafting a compelling plotline is one of the most important and challenging aspects of writing a novel or short story. A good plotline should keep readers engaged and eager to turn the page, while also providing enough twists and turns to keep them guessing. So how do you create a plotline that will keep readers on the edge of their seats?

▸ **Start with the end in mind:** Before you begin writing, it's important to have a clear idea of where your story is headed. What is the ultimate goal or conflict that your protagonist will face? What are the stakes if they fail? Having a clear endpoint in mind will help you stay focused as you write and ensure that your story stays on track.

▸ **Create believable characters:** Your characters are the driving force behind your plot, so it's essential that they feel real and fully developed. Spend time getting to know your protagonist and their motivations, fears, and flaws. The more complex and relatable your characters are, the more invested readers will be in their journey.

▸ **Establish conflict early on:** A good plotline needs conflict to keep things interesting. Whether it's a personal struggle or an external obstacle, your protagonist should face challenges from the very beginning of your story. This will create tension and keep readers engaged as they follow your character's journey.

▸ **Use the "Yes, but/No, and" method:** This technique is a great way to keep your story moving forward and avoid getting stuck in a rut. Essentially, it involves presenting your protagonist with a choice or obstacle, then following it up with a "Yes, but" or "No, and" that complicates the situation. This keeps the story moving forward and creates a sense of momentum.

▸ **Add unexpected twists and turns:** A good plotline should keep readers guessing and surprised. Consider adding unexpected twists or turns that will catch readers off guard and keep them engaged. Just be careful not to rely too heavily on cliches or cheap plot devices.

▸ **Keep the pacing in mind:** A well-crafted plotline should have a steady pace that keeps readers engaged without feeling rushed. Think about the balance between action, dialogue, and description in your story, and make sure that each scene serves a purpose in advancing the plot.

▸ **Tie up loose ends:** As your story nears its conclusion, make sure that all loose ends are tied up and any unanswered questions are resolved. This will give readers a sense of closure and satisfaction as they finish the book.

Crafting a compelling plotline takes time and effort. Don't be afraid to revise and tweak as you go along, and don't get discouraged if things don't go exactly as planned. With patience and perseverance, you can create a story that will captivate readers and leave them eager for more.

Use Conflict to Move Your Story Forward

Conflict is an essential element of a compelling story. It's what keeps the reader engaged and interested, and it's what drives the plot forward. Without conflict, a story would be flat, uninteresting, and ultimately forgettable. As a writer, it's your job to create conflict that is both believable and engaging.

Conflict can come in many forms. It can be a disagreement between two characters, a struggle against an external force, or an internal battle within a character's own mind. Whatever form it takes, conflict is what makes a story exciting and memorable.

One way to create conflict is to give your characters opposing goals. For example, if one character wants to achieve something that another character wants to prevent, conflict is almost guaranteed to arise. This can be as simple as a protagonist trying to save a kidnapped victim while the antagonist tries to stop them, or as complex as two characters with different ideologies clashing over a moral issue.

Another way to create conflict is to give your characters flaws that lead to problems. For example, if your protagonist is impulsive and tends to act without thinking, this can create problems and conflicts throughout the story. Their impulsiveness could cause them to make poor decisions, putting themselves and others in danger. This could also lead to conflict with other characters who are more cautious or rational.

External forces can also be used to create conflict. This could be anything from a natural disaster to an invading army. These types of conflicts can be particularly effective in creating tension and suspense, as the characters are faced with an obstacle that seems insurmountable.

When creating conflict, it's important to make sure it's believable and organic. The conflict should arise naturally from the story and the characters, rather than feeling forced or contrived. It should also be resolved in a satisfying way, with the characters either overcoming the conflict or coming to a new understanding.

One of the best ways to create conflict is to put yourself in your characters' shoes. Think about what you would do if you were in their situation. What conflicts would arise? What obstacles would you face? What would you do to overcome them? By understanding your characters' motivations and goals, you can create conflicts that are true to their personalities and experiences.

In addition to creating conflict, it's important to balance it with other elements of storytelling, such as character development and setting. Too much conflict can be overwhelming and exhausting for the reader, while too little can make the story feel flat and uninteresting.

Overall, conflict is a crucial element of a compelling story. It's what keeps the reader engaged and invested in the characters and the plot. As a writer, it's your job to create conflict that is both believable and engaging, and to use it to drive the story forward in a way that is satisfying and meaningful.

Research, Research, Research

Writing fiction is an art form that requires a combination of creativity and research to create a believable and engaging story. While some writers may be tempted to take artistic liberties with their settings and characters, it's important to research thoroughly to ensure accuracy and authenticity. By taking the time to conduct research, writers can create a more immersive and engaging world for their readers.

One of the most important aspects of researching for fiction writing is to familiarize oneself with the setting of the story. Whether it's a real-world location or a fictional one, understanding the geography, culture, and history of the setting is essential to creating a believable and immersive world. This may involve reading books, watching documentaries, or even visiting the location in person.

Similarly, research into the characters themselves is equally important. Writers should strive to create characters that are realistic and well-rounded, with a unique set of personality traits, motivations, and flaws. Conducting research into the experiences and backgrounds of characters can help writers to better understand their actions and motivations, and can lead to a more complex and nuanced portrayal.

In addition to researching the setting and characters, writers should also consider the time period in which their story is set. Depending on the time period, there may be certain cultural or societal norms that need to be taken into account. For example, a story set in the Victorian era would likely require research into the etiquette and customs of the time, while a story set in a post-apocalyptic world may require research into survival skills and strategies.

It's important to note that research does not necessarily have to be a chore. In fact, many writers (including this one) find that the research process can be incredibly rewarding and inspiring. By immersing oneself in the world of the story, writers can gain a deeper understanding of their characters and setting, and may even uncover new ideas and plot twists.

Of course, it's important to use caution when conducting research, particularly when it comes to sensitive or controversial topics. Writers should always be mindful of cultural appropriation and the potential for perpetuating harmful stereotypes. Additionally, it's important to fact-check any information gathered during research to ensure accuracy.

Research is a vital aspect of fiction writing that should not be overlooked. By taking the time to familiarize oneself with the setting, characters, and time period of a story, writers can create a more immersive and believable world for their readers. Through research, writers can gain a deeper understanding of their characters and setting, and may even uncover new ideas and plot twists. So, whether you're writing historical fiction, science fiction, or anything in between, be sure to research thoroughly to ensure accuracy and authenticity in your writing.

Practice Empathy to Create Awesome Characters

Creating complex and relatable characters is a key aspect of writing fiction. As a writer, it's important to understand your characters and to make them feel like real people with their own unique personalities, flaws, and motivations. To achieve this, practicing empathy can be an essential tool.

Empathy is the ability to understand and share the feelings of others. It's a skill that writers can use to create well-rounded and believable characters. By empathizing with your characters, you can create a deeper understanding of their experiences, thoughts, and emotions. This, in turn, can help you write more nuanced and layered characters that readers can connect with on a deeper level.

To practice empathy in your writing, you need to start by understanding your characters' backgrounds, personalities, and motivations. Think about their childhoods, their relationships, their fears, and their dreams. Consider how these things have shaped them into the people they are today. Use this information to create fully-realized characters that readers can relate to and empathize with.

One way to develop empathy for your characters is to put yourself in their shoes. Imagine how they would feel in a particular situation, and try to see things from their perspective. Ask yourself questions like "What would it be like to be in their position?" and "How would I feel if this happened to me?"

Another way to practice empathy is to draw from your own experiences. Think about times when you've felt similar emotions or faced similar challenges as your characters. Use these experiences to add depth and authenticity to your characters' feelings and reactions.

When it comes to writing dialogue, practicing empathy can help you create authentic and believable conversations. Think about how your characters would speak and the words they would use based on their backgrounds and personalities. Pay attention to the way people talk in real life, and use this as a guide for writing natural-sounding dialogue.

It's also important to remember that not all characters will have the same experiences or perspectives as you. Writing characters from diverse backgrounds and experiences can be challenging, but it's essential for creating a rich and inclusive story. To write diverse characters, it's important to do your research and to consult with people who have firsthand experience with the issues you're addressing.

In addition to creating complex and relatable characters, practicing empathy can also help you craft more engaging and meaningful stories. By empathizing with your characters, you can create deeper and more meaningful conflicts and themes. These elements can make your story more compelling and impactful for readers.

Practicing empathy is an essential tool for creating fully-realized and relatable characters in fiction writing. By understanding your characters' backgrounds, motivations, and perspectives, you can write more nuanced and layered stories that connect with readers on a deeper level. Use empathy to create authentic dialogue and to address diverse perspectives and experiences. By doing so, you'll be on your way to becoming a better fiction writer.

Make Your Hero Believable and Vulnerable

Ah, the hero. The protagonist of our stories, the one we root for, the one we want to see triumph in the end. But what makes a hero truly great? Is it their unwavering strength and unflappable courage, or is there something more to it? As an aspiring writer, it's important to remember that the most memorable heroes are those that are both believable and vulnerable.

Believability is key when it comes to crafting a great hero (or heroes). Your readers need to be able to identify with your protagonist on some level, to see themselves in their struggles and triumphs. This means creating a character that feels real, with flaws and quirks and imperfections just like the rest of us.

One way to make your hero more believable is to give them a relatable backstory. What challenges have they faced in their life that have shaped who they are today? What motivates them to keep going, even when things seem impossible? By giving your hero a rich history, you help to ground them in reality and make them more relatable to your readers.

Another way to make your hero more believable is to give them realistic strengths and weaknesses. Yes, they may be the protagonist, but that doesn't mean they're invincible. Your hero should have skills and talents that set them apart, but they should also have flaws that make them more human. Maybe they're a skilled fighter, but they struggle with trust issues. Maybe they're a brilliant strategist, but they have a tendency to be reckless. Whatever the case may be, giving your hero a balance of strengths and weaknesses will help make them more believable.

But believability alone isn't enough to make a hero truly great. They also need to be vulnerable. This means putting them in situations where they're not always in control, where they have to make difficult choices and face tough consequences. It means giving them emotional depth, so that readers can connect with them on a deeper level.

One way to make your hero more vulnerable is to give them internal conflicts. Maybe they're struggling with a decision that could have serious consequences, or maybe they're dealing with unresolved trauma from their past. By giving your hero internal struggles, you not only make them more relatable, but you also create opportunities for character growth and development.

Another way to make your hero more vulnerable is to put them in physical danger. Yes, they may be brave and capable, but that doesn't mean they're invincible. By putting your hero in situations where they could be hurt or even killed, you create tension and suspense that will keep your readers on the edge of their seats.

Ultimately, creating a great hero is all about balance. You need to make them believable, with a relatable backstory, realistic strengths and weaknesses, and internal conflicts. But you also need to make them vulnerable, by putting them in situations where they're not always in control and where they face real consequences. By striking this balance, you create a hero that readers will truly care about, one that they'll root for until the very end.

If you want to create a truly great hero, remember to make them both believable and vulnerable. Give them a backstory that feels real, with strengths and weaknesses that make them human. Put them in situations where they're not always in control, where they have to make difficult choices and face tough consequences. By doing so, you'll create a hero that readers will truly care about, one that will stay with them long after the story is over.

Everyone Loves a Villain

Is there anything more alluring in fiction than a truly great antagonist? From Darth Vader to Hannibal Lecter to Voldemort, a good villain can elevate a story from merely entertaining to downright unforgettable. There's something about a well-crafted baddie that speaks to our primal instincts, that draws us in and keeps us hooked.

But what is it that makes a great villain? Is it their menacing presence, their twisted motivations, or the chaos they create? In truth, it's a little bit of everything, but the most important thing is that they feel real. A great villain isn't just evil for the sake of being evil; they have reasons for doing what they do, even if those reasons are deeply misguided.

As an aspiring writer, creating a truly memorable villain can be a daunting task. After all, you don't want them to come across as cartoonish or one-dimensional. You want your readers to understand them, to feel for them (even if they don't necessarily agree with their actions). So, where do you start?

The first thing to consider is your villain's backstory. What made them the way they are? Did they suffer some great trauma, or were they simply born with a twisted worldview? Whatever the case may be, it's important to flesh out your villain's past in order to make them feel like a real, three-dimensional character.

Once you have a handle on your villain's backstory, it's time to start thinking about their motivations. What do they want, and why do they want it? Remember, a great villain is never evil just for the sake of being evil; they have goals and desires, just like any other character. It's up to you, the writer, to figure out what those goals are and how they inform your villain's actions.

Another key element to consider is your villain's relationship with your protagonist. Are they mortal enemies, locked in a battle for the fate of the world? Or are they more subtle foes, working behind the scenes to thwart your hero's plans? Whatever the case may be, it's important to establish the dynamic between your villain and your protagonist early on in your story. This will help build tension and keep your readers engaged.

Of course, creating a great villain is only half the battle. You also need to know how to write them effectively. One key tip is to avoid making your villain too over-the-top. Yes, they may be evil, but they shouldn't be a caricature. Give them some nuance, some depth, and your readers will be more invested in the story.

Another important thing to keep in mind is that your villain should be a worthy adversary for your protagonist. They should pose a real threat, both physically and emotionally. If your villain is too weak or too easily defeated, your readers won't feel any sense of satisfaction when they're finally vanquished. On the other hand, if your villain is too powerful, your readers may start to lose faith in your hero's ability to prevail.

Ultimately, creating a great villain is all about balance. You need to give them enough depth and nuance to make them feel real, but you also need to make sure they pose a real threat to your hero. With a little bit of planning and a lot of creativity, you can create a villain that will go down in literary history.

Give Your Characters Memorable Names

One of the most important elements of a good story is the characters. They are the heart and soul of any narrative, and their names play a significant role in how they are perceived by the reader. A character's name can convey a lot about their personality, background, and motivations. Therefore, it's crucial to create memorable and unique character names that suit the tone and genre of your story.

When creating character names, there are several factors to consider. The first is the tone of your story. Are you writing a dark, gritty crime thriller or a light-hearted romantic comedy? The tone of your story will have a significant impact on the names you choose for your characters. For example, if you're writing a horror story, you might want to choose names that are ominous or foreboding, such as Raven, Cain, or Lilith. On the other hand, if you're writing a romance novel, you might choose names that are romantic and poetic, such as Juliet, Tristan, or Aurora.

Another factor to consider is the genre of your story. Different genres have different conventions when it comes to naming characters. For example, in fantasy and science fiction, character names often have a more otherworldly or futuristic feel. Names like Arwen, Legolas, and Galadriel from "The Lord of the Rings" trilogy or Neo, Trinity, and Morpheus from "The Matrix" are good examples of this. In contrast, in a realistic, contemporary story, you might want to choose names that are more common and familiar, such as Emma, Jack, or Sarah.

It's also important to consider the cultural background of your characters. Depending on their nationality or ethnicity, their names may reflect certain traditions or cultural values. For example, if you're writing a story set in Japan, you might choose names like Sakura, Takeshi, or Yuki. If you're writing a story set in India, you might choose names like Ravi, Priya, or Amit. By researching and choosing culturally appropriate names, you can add authenticity and depth to your characters.

When creating character names, it's important to make them memorable and unique. A unique name can make a character stand out in the reader's mind, making them more memorable and engaging. However, it's important not to go overboard with unusual spellings or overly complicated names, as this can be distracting and confusing. A good rule of thumb is to choose names that are easy to pronounce and remember, but still unique and distinctive.

One way to create unique character names is to use variations of common names. For example, instead of naming your character John, you might choose a variation like Jonathon, Jaxon, or Johanna. Another approach is to combine two names to create something new, like Serenity or Jaxon.

In addition to considering the tone, genre, cultural background, and uniqueness of your character names, it's also important to make sure they are appropriate for the story and the character's personality. A name that doesn't fit a character's personality can be jarring and take the reader out of the story. For example, if you have a character who is shy and introverted, a name like Blaze or Maverick might not be appropriate.

Creating memorable and unique character names is an essential part of writing a good story. By considering the tone, genre, cultural background, uniqueness, and appropriateness of your character names, you can create characters that are engaging, authentic, and memorable. So the next time you're naming your characters, take the time to choose names that suit them and your story.

Experiment with Different Points of View

As a fiction writer, one of the most important decisions you'll make is deciding on the point of view from which to tell your story. Point of view, or POV, refers to the perspective from which a story is narrated. There are many different points of view to choose from, each with its own advantages and challenges. By experimenting with different points of view, you can find the one that works best for your story and writing style.

One common point of view is first-person, in which the narrator is a character in the story and tells the story from their own perspective. First-person POV can create a sense of intimacy and immediacy, allowing readers to connect with the narrator on a personal level. However, it can also limit the scope of the story, as the narrator can only report on what they directly experience or observe. Additionally, first-person POV can be challenging to maintain over a long story, as the narrator's voice must be consistent throughout.

Another common point of view is third-person limited, in which the narrator is not a character in the story but is able to see into the thoughts and emotions of one character at a time. Third-person limited POV can provide a broader view of the story than first-person, while still allowing readers to connect with the characters on a personal level. It can also allow for multiple narrators or perspectives, which can add complexity and depth to the story. However, it can be challenging to maintain a consistent tone and voice, and switching between narrators can be disorienting for readers.

A third point of view is omniscient, in which the narrator is all-knowing and can see into the thoughts and emotions of all characters in the story. Omniscient POV can provide a broad, sweeping view of the story, and can allow for commentary and analysis that other POVs don't allow. However, it can also be distancing for readers, as they may not feel as connected to the characters as they would with first-person or third-person limited POV. Additionally, omniscient POV can be challenging to maintain, as the narrator must balance multiple perspectives and voices.

In addition to the traditional POVs, there are also less commonly used ones that can add a fresh twist to your story. For example, you could experiment with second-person POV, in which the narrator addresses the reader directly ("You walk into the room and see..."). This can create a sense of immediacy and immersion, but can also be challenging to maintain over a long story.

Ultimately, the key to using POV effectively is to remain consistent and clear throughout the story. Whether you choose first-person, third-person limited, omniscient, or another POV entirely, make sure you establish the rules of your POV early on and stick to them throughout.

Each story or book has its own unique requirements, and the POV you choose should serve the narrative and its characters. By experimenting with different POVs, you can gain a better understanding of how each one works and how it can be used to enhance your storytelling.

Employ the Active Voice

When it comes to writing, one of the most important aspects to consider is the voice in which you write. Specifically, the choice between active and passive voice can make a huge difference in the effectiveness of your writing. Active voice is generally considered to be more engaging and clear than passive voice, and it's important to understand why and how to use it effectively.

Active voice is a type of sentence structure in which the subject of the sentence performs the action. For example, "John ate the pizza." In this sentence, "John" is the subject and "ate" is the action. Passive voice, on the other hand, is a sentence structure in which the subject is being acted upon. For example, "The pizza was eaten by John." In this sentence, "pizza" is the subject and "was eaten" is the action.

So why is active voice considered to be more engaging and effective than passive voice? There are a few reasons. First, active voice is more direct and clear. It makes it immediately clear who is performing the action in the sentence. This helps the reader to follow the story or argument more easily.

Second, active voice is more engaging and dynamic. It creates a sense of action and movement in the sentence. It can help to make your writing more interesting and compelling to read.

Finally, active voice is more concise than passive voice. Passive voice often requires more words to express the same idea, which can make writing feel clunky and overly complicated.

So, how can you use active voice effectively in your writing?

▸ **Identify the subject and verb:** In order to use active voice, it's important to identify the subject and verb in each sentence. Ask yourself, "Who or what is performing the action?" and "What action are they performing?"

▸ **Rearrange the sentence:** Once you have identified the subject and verb, rearrange the sentence so that the subject comes first, followed by the verb. This will help you to create active voice sentences.

▸ **Use strong verbs:** Using strong, action-oriented verbs can help to make your writing more dynamic and engaging. Instead of saying "The car was driven by Michael," try "Michael drove the car." This not only puts the focus on the subject, but also uses a more active verb.

▸ **Avoid passive constructions:** Be aware of constructions that are inherently passive, such as "it was decided" or "it was found." Instead, use active verbs to convey the same meaning.

▸ **Use active voice in dialogue:** Active voice is particularly effective in dialogue, as it can help to create a sense of immediacy and action in the conversation.

Using an active voice can make a huge difference in the effectiveness of your writing. It draws your readers in and makes them want to read the next sentence. Take a look at something you wrote recently ... did you use the passive voice in any parts, even unintentionally? If so, try rewriting it using your active voice.

Show, Don't Tell

One of the most common pieces of advice given to writers is to "show, not tell." It's a simple phrase, but it can be difficult to put into practice. Essentially, this advice means that instead of telling the reader what is happening in your story or essay, you should use descriptive details and sensory language to create a vivid image that allows the reader to experience it for themselves.

Mark Twain has a great quote about this. "Don't say the old lady screamed," he said. "Bring her on and let her scream!"

When you "show" instead of "tell," you engage the reader's imagination and allow them to become fully immersed in your story. This makes for a much more engaging and memorable reading experience.

One way to "show" is to use sensory details. For example, instead of saying "The room was cold," you could say "I could see my breath in the air, and my fingers felt numb." This creates a much more vivid image in the reader's mind and allows them to experience the cold alongside the narrator.

Another way to "show" is to use dialogue and actions to reveal character traits and emotions. Instead of saying "She was angry," you could have the character clench their fists, their face turning red, and have them snap at another character. This way, the reader can see the anger for themselves and draw their own conclusions about the character's personality.

When you "tell" instead of "show," you risk losing your reader's interest. For example, if you write "The boy was sad," the reader may feel disconnected from the character and their emotions. But if you write "The boy's eyes filled with tears, and his shoulders slumped," the reader can better empathize with the character and feel more invested in the story.

Of course, there are times when telling is appropriate, especially when summarizing or providing necessary information. But in general, "showing" is a much more effective way to engage your reader and bring your writing to life.

One common mistake writers make when trying to "show" is over-describing or over-explaining. It's important to strike a balance between providing enough detail to create a vivid image and leaving room for the reader's imagination to fill in the gaps. This can take practice and feedback from other writers or readers.

Another challenge with "showing" is that it can be more time-consuming and require more careful thought and attention to detail than simply telling. But the effort is well worth it when it comes to creating a powerful and engaging piece of writing.

"Show, don't tell" is a fundamental principle of good writing. By using descriptive details, sensory language, dialogue, and actions, you can bring your writing to life and create a more engaging reading experience. Remember to strike a balance between providing enough detail and leaving room for the reader's imagination.

Use Strong Verbs and Avoid Adverbs

When it comes to writing, the words you choose are incredibly important. Strong verbs can add power, impact, and specificity to your writing, while adverbs can often detract from these qualities. As Ernest Hemingway said, "it is the nouns and verbs, not the adjectives and adverbs, which make sentences live."

First, let's talk about verbs. A verb is a word that expresses an action, occurrence, or state of being. Strong verbs are verbs that are specific, powerful, and vivid. They can help bring your writing to life by providing a clear picture of what is happening. For example, instead of using a weak verb like "walked," you could use a stronger verb like "strolled," "marched," or "sauntered." Each of these verbs conveys a different image and creates a different tone for your writing.

Then there are adverbs. Adverbs are words that modify verbs, adjectives, or other adverbs. They are often used to add information about how something is done, but they can also be used to add emphasis or to clarify meaning. While adverbs can be useful in certain situations, they are often overused and can detract from the impact of your writing. For example, instead of using an adverb like "quickly" to modify a verb like "ran," you could use a stronger verb like "sprinted" or "darted." This not only adds specificity to your writing but also eliminates the need for an adverb.

Why is it important to use strong verbs and avoid adverbs?

‣ **Strong verbs make your writing more engaging:** When you use strong verbs, you create a more vivid picture of what is happening. This can make your writing more interesting and engaging for your readers.

‣ **Strong verbs help you avoid cliches:** When you rely too heavily on adverbs, you run the risk of falling into cliched language. By using strong verbs, you can avoid these common phrases and create fresh, original language.

‣ **Adverbs can be unnecessary:** Adverbs are often used to add information that could be conveyed more effectively with a strong verb. By eliminating adverbs and using strong verbs instead, you can make your writing more concise and impactful.

These are skills that you can improve at with minimal practice. Here's some tips:

✓**Choose strong verbs that convey specific actions or emotions:** Instead of relying on weak verbs and adverbs, try to find verbs that convey a specific image or emotion. For example, instead of saying "he walked quickly," you could say "he raced" or "he sprinted."

✓**Use descriptive language to convey meaning:** Instead of relying on adverbs to convey meaning, try to use descriptive language to paint a picture for your readers. For example, instead of saying "she spoke loudly," you could say "her voice boomed across the room."

✓**Edit out unnecessary adverbs:** When you're editing your writing, pay close attention to any adverbs you've used. Ask yourself whether they are really necessary, or whether a strong verb could convey the same meaning more effectively.

Using strong verbs and avoiding adverbs is an important part of creating powerful, impactful writing. By choosing strong verbs that convey specific actions or emotions, using descriptive language to convey meaning, and editing out unnecessary adverbs, you can create writing that is engaging, concise, and memorable.

"Dialogue is a Powerful Weapon."

Dialogue is perhaps the most powerful tools a writer has in their arsenal. It allows readers to learn more about characters, their personalities, and their relationships with one another. Additionally, dialogue can move the story forward and create tension, conflict, and suspense. Whether you're writing a novel, short story, or screenplay, mastering the art of dialogue is crucial to creating a compelling and engaging story.

First and foremost, dialogue is a great way to develop characters. It allows you to reveal their personalities, quirks, and backstory. For example, a character's use of slang or regional dialect can provide insight into their background and where they come from. Additionally, the way a character speaks and interacts with others can reveal their personality traits, such as shyness, confidence, or aggressiveness.

Dialogue can also be used to reveal character relationships. A character's choice of words and the way they speak to others can reveal a lot about their feelings towards that person. For example, a character who speaks harshly or sarcastically to someone may be harboring resentment or anger towards them. Conversely, a character who speaks gently or supportively to someone may have positive feelings towards them.

Dialogue can move the story forward. Dialogue can be used to create conflict and tension, which can help propel the story forward. For example, a heated argument between two characters can create tension and keep the reader engaged. Additionally, dialogue can be used to reveal important plot points, such as a character's motivation or a key piece of information.

When writing dialogue, it's important to keep a few things in mind. First, make sure that your dialogue sounds natural and realistic. Avoid using overly formal language or dialogue that feels forced. Instead, try to write dialogue that sounds like something real people would say. One way to do this is to listen to the way people talk in real life and use that as a basis for your writing.

Another important aspect of dialogue is that it should be purposeful. Every line of dialogue should have a reason for being there. Whether it's to reveal something about a character or to move the plot forward, every line of dialogue should serve a purpose.

Finally, it's important to remember that dialogue should be balanced with narrative description. Too much dialogue can make a story feel flat, while too much narrative can make a story feel sluggish. By finding the right balance between dialogue and narrative, you can create a story that is both engaging, realistic and well-paced.

Pacing Creates Tension and Suspense

One of the most critical skills you need to master is the ability to create tension and suspense in your writing. By manipulating the pace of your story, you can make your readers feel more engaged, invested, and eager to turn the next page.

Pacing is all about how quickly or slowly events unfold in your story. Depending on the type of story you're telling, you may want to vary the pace to create different effects. For example, if you're writing a thriller or a mystery, you may want to keep the pace fast and intense to keep your readers on the edge of their seats. Conversely, if you're writing a more introspective or character-driven story, you may want to slow down the pace to allow your readers to reflect on the character's thoughts and emotions.

Here's how to use pacing effectively in your writing:

▸ **Start with a hook:** The opening of your story should be attention-grabbing and exciting. You want to draw your readers in and make them curious about what's going to happen next.

▸ **Vary sentence length:** Short, snappy sentences can create a sense of urgency and excitement, while longer, more complex sentences can slow things down and allow you to explore your character's thoughts and feelings in more detail.

▸ **Use cliffhangers:** Ending a chapter or section with a cliffhanger can create a sense of anticipation and make your readers eager to find out what happens next.

▸ **Build up to the climax:** The climax of your story should be the most intense and exciting part. You want to build up to it gradually, creating tension and suspense along the way.

▸ **Use dialogue:** Dialogue can be a powerful tool for pacing. It can help to break up long passages of description or introspection and create a more dynamic and engaging reading experience.

▸ **Use action scenes:** Action scenes can be great for keeping the pace fast and exciting. Just be sure to balance them with moments of reflection and character development.

▸ **Don't rush:** While it's essential to keep the pace moving, you don't want to rush through important moments in your story. Take the time to explore your character's thoughts and emotions and create a rich, immersive world for your readers.

By using pacing effectively, you can create a more engaging and exciting reading experience for your audience. Whether you're writing a thriller, a romance, or a literary novel, mastering the art of pacing can help take your writing to the next level.

Sensory Details are Immersive

Writing is all about creating a vivid and engaging experience for your reader. One of the most effective ways to do this is by incorporating sensory details into your writing. Sensory details are descriptive words and phrases that engage the reader's senses - sight, sound, touch, taste, and smell. By using sensory details, you can transport your reader into the scene and immerse them in the story.

To start, it's important to understand the five senses and how to incorporate them into your writing.

1. ***Sight*** - When using sight, think about the colors, shapes, and textures in your scene. What does your character see? Is it a bright, sunny day or a dark and stormy night? What is the landscape like? Are there mountains, forests, or oceans in the distance? By painting a picture with your words, you can bring your reader right into the scene.

2. ***Sound*** - Sound can be used to set the mood of a scene or to create tension. Are there birds chirping in the trees or dogs barking in the distance? Is there a loud bang that startles your character or the sound of a soothing melody playing in the

background? By using sound, you can create a more immersive experience for your reader.

3. **Touch** - When using touch, think about the textures and temperatures in your scene. What does your character feel? Is the ground rough or smooth beneath their feet? Is the air hot and humid or cold and crisp? By incorporating touch, you can help your reader feel as if they are physically present in the scene.

4. **Taste** - Taste is often overlooked in writing, but it can be a powerful tool for creating a sense of realism. Think about the flavors and textures of the food your character is eating or the drinks they are drinking. Are they savoring a rich, chocolatey dessert or sipping on a refreshing, citrusy cocktail? By including taste, you can help your reader experience the scene more fully.

5. **Smell** - Smell can be used to create a sense of atmosphere and mood. What does your character smell? Is there a strong scent of pine trees in the air or the faint hint of jasmine? By using smell, you can transport your reader to the scene and help them feel as if they are truly there.

Here are some pointers to help you use sensory details effectively:

▸ **Use sensory details to create a strong sense of atmosphere.** By using specific details, you can transport your reader to the scene and help them feel as if they are truly there.

▸ **Use sensory details to create tension or suspense.** By using sound or touch, you can create a sense of danger or unease that keeps your reader engaged.

▸ **Use sensory details to create a sense of character.** By describing what your character sees, hears, smells, tastes, and touches, you can help your reader understand who they are and what they're going through.

▸ **Use sensory details sparingly.** While sensory details can be powerful, it's important not to overdo it. Too many details can overwhelm your reader and detract from the story.

▸ **Use sensory details to create contrast.** By contrasting different senses, you can create a sense of surprise or interest. For example, describing a beautiful, sunny day with the sound of thunder in the distance can create a sense of tension and excitement.

By engaging the reader's senses, you can create a more immersive experience and bring your story to life. So next time you're writing, think about the five senses and how you can incorporate them into your work. Help your readers see, hear, touch, taste and smell your amazing story!

Proper Grammar and Punctuation

Good writing is not only about having great ideas, but also about being able to express them clearly and effectively. One of the keys to achieving this is to use proper grammar and punctuation. Although it may seem like a small detail, correct grammar and punctuation can have a big impact on the readability and professionalism of your writing.

Grammar refers to the rules that govern the structure of sentences, including the proper use of nouns, verbs, adjectives, adverbs, and other parts of speech. Punctuation refers to the symbols used to indicate pauses, emphasis, and other aspects of sentence structure, such as commas, periods, semicolons, and colons.

Here are some tips for using proper grammar and punctuation in your writing:

- **Know the basics:** Make sure you have a good understanding of basic grammar and punctuation rules, such as subject-verb agreement, proper use of pronouns, and common punctuation marks.

- **Proofread your work:** Always take the time to proofread your writing for grammar and punctuation errors. Read through your work carefully, and consider using a grammar and spell-checking tool to catch any mistakes you may have missed.
- **Avoid common mistakes:** Watch out for common grammar and punctuation errors, such as using apostrophes incorrectly or misusing commas.
- **Use consistent style:** Consistency is key when it comes to grammar and punctuation. Choose a style guide (such as the Chicago Manual of Style or the AP Stylebook) and stick to it throughout your writing.
- **Don't overuse punctuation:** While punctuation is important for conveying meaning, it's also possible to overdo it. Use punctuation marks sparingly and only when they are necessary.
- **Use proper capitalization:** Make sure to capitalize proper nouns (such as names, places, and titles) and the first word of every sentence.
- **Learn from your mistakes:** If you do make a grammar or punctuation error, take note of it and learn from it. Use your mistakes as an opportunity to improve your writing skills.

Using proper grammar and punctuation is not only important for the readability of your writing, but it also shows a level of professionalism and attention to detail. Good grammar and punctuation can help you convey your ideas more effectively, and can even help you avoid confusion and misunderstandings. Avid readers don't like sloppy writing!

One of the best ways to improve your grammar and punctuation skills is to read widely and often. When you read, pay attention to the way sentences are structured and punctuated. This can help you internalize the rules of grammar and punctuation and apply them to your own writing.

In addition, there are many resources available to help you improve your grammar and punctuation skills. Online grammar and punctuation guides, YouTube, writing blogs, and even college courses can help you learn the rules and practice applying them to your own writing.

Readers Like Paragraph Breaks

When it comes to writing, it's not just the words on the page that matter. The way those words are presented can make a big difference in how your writing is received by readers. That's where paragraph breaks come in. They might seem like a small thing, but they play a big role in making your writing easier to read and understand.

A paragraph break is simply a blank line between two blocks of text. It's a way of signaling to the reader that you're moving on to a new thought or idea. When used effectively, paragraph breaks can help your writing flow smoothly and guide your reader through your ideas.

One of the main benefits of using paragraph breaks is that they make your writing easier to read. If you present your ideas in large blocks of text with no breaks, your reader can quickly become overwhelmed and lose interest. By breaking up your writing into smaller chunks, you make it more approachable and easier to digest.

Paragraph breaks also help to organize your writing. By grouping related ideas together in a single paragraph, you create a clear structure that guides the reader through your thought process. When you're writing, try to limit each paragraph to one central idea or argument. This makes it easier for your reader to follow along and understand your point of view.

Another benefit of paragraph breaks is that they help to create emphasis and rhythm in your writing. By using short paragraphs for important or dramatic moments, you can make those moments stand out and give them added weight. On the other hand, longer paragraphs can create a slower, more contemplative tone that's appropriate for reflective or introspective writing.

In addition to using paragraph breaks to break up your writing into smaller chunks, there are a few other things to keep in mind when using this technique. First, make sure to use consistent formatting throughout your writing. This means using the same amount of space between each paragraph and using the same font and size.

Second, use paragraph breaks sparingly. While they're a great tool for making your writing easier to read, too many breaks can actually have the opposite effect. If you use too many breaks, your writing can start to feel choppy and disjointed. Use breaks strategically to guide your reader through your writing, but don't overdo it.

Finally, make sure to use paragraph breaks in a way that makes sense for your writing. Different types of writing, such as academic papers, creative writing, or business writing, may have different conventions when it comes to paragraph breaks. Make sure to research and understand the conventions of your specific genre or audience to make sure your writing is effective and professional.

Descriptive Adjectives Add Depth

Writing is a powerful tool that allows us to communicate our thoughts, feelings, and ideas to others. However, not all writing is created equal. Some writing can leave a lasting impression, while others fall flat. One way to make your writing stand out is to use descriptive adjectives. These little words can add depth and color to your writing, making it more engaging and interesting for your readers. In this article, we will explore the importance of using descriptive adjectives and provide tips on how to use them effectively.

Descriptive adjectives are words that modify or describe nouns and pronouns, adding detail and depth to them. They help to paint a vivid picture in the reader's mind, allowing them to see, hear, taste, smell, and feel what the writer is trying to convey. For example, instead of saying "I saw a car," you could say "I saw a sleek, black sports car," which gives the reader a more specific and detailed image.

One of the benefits of using descriptive adjectives is that it can make your writing more engaging and interesting. When you use descriptive adjectives, you create a mental image in the reader's mind, which can help to hold their attention and keep them interested in what you are writing. This is particularly important if you are trying to persuade or entertain your readers, as it can help to make your writing more effective.

Another benefit of using descriptive adjectives is that it can make your writing more memorable. When you use vivid and colorful language, it can leave a lasting impression on the reader, making your writing more memorable and impactful. This is particularly important if you are writing a story or essay that you want your readers to remember long after they have finished reading it.

How can you use descriptive adjectives effectively in your writing? Here are some tips:

- **Be specific:** Use adjectives that are specific and precise. Instead of saying "the house was big," you could say "the house was a sprawling, three-story mansion."

- **Use sensory language:** Use adjectives that appeal to the senses. For example, instead of saying "the air was cold," you could say "the air was crisp and icy."

- **Use comparisons:** Use adjectives that compare one thing to another. For example, instead of saying "the dress was pretty," you could say "the dress was as lovely as a summer sunset."

- **Avoid overuse:** While descriptive adjectives can be effective, it's important not to overuse them. Too many adjectives can make your writing seem cluttered and overwhelming. Use them sparingly and only when necessary.

- **Vary your language:** Don't rely on the same adjectives over and over again. Use a variety of adjectives to keep your writing interesting and engaging.

Using descriptive adjectives can add depth and color to your writing, making it more engaging, interesting, and memorable for your readers. They can help you create vivid mental images that will stay with your readers long after they have finished reading.

Avoid Ugly Words and Ugly Language Tags

Writing is a powerful tool that allows us to communicate our thoughts, feelings, and ideas to others. However, not all writing is created equal. Some writing can be beautiful and uplifting, while others can be ugly and unpleasant. As a writer, it's important to be mindful of the words and language tags we use, as they can have a significant impact on the tone and effectiveness of our writing. In this article, we will explore why writers should avoid ugly words and language tags and provide tips on how to use more positive and uplifting language in your writing.

First and foremost, it's important to define what we mean by "ugly" words and language tags. Ugly words are those that have a negative connotation or are associated with unpleasant feelings or experiences. Examples of ugly words include slurs, curses, and derogatory terms. Language tags, on the other hand, are words or phrases that are used to describe or categorize people or things. Examples of ugly language tags include labels such as "fat," "ugly," or "stupid."

One reason why writers should avoid using ugly words and language tags is that they can be hurtful and offensive to readers. Using derogatory language can make readers feel uncomfortable or attacked, which can undermine the effectiveness of your writing. It's important to be respectful of your readers and to avoid using language that could be seen as discriminatory or prejudiced.

How can writers use more positive and uplifting language in their writing?

- ▸ **Use descriptive language:** Instead of using ugly language tags, use descriptive language that focuses on the positive qualities of a person or thing. For example, instead of calling someone "fat," you could describe them as "curvy" or "shapely."
- ▸ **Use positive language:** Instead of focusing on the negative, use positive language to inspire and uplift your readers. For example, instead of saying "don't be lazy," you could say "be proactive and productive."
- ▸ **Avoid stereotypes:** Avoid using stereotypes or generalizations that can be offensive or hurtful. Instead, focus on the individual qualities and experiences of the people or things you are writing about.
- ▸ **Be respectful:** Always be respectful of your readers and avoid using language that could be seen as discriminatory or prejudiced. Use inclusive language that acknowledges and respects the diversity of your readership.
- ▸ **Use humor:** Humor can be a powerful tool to lighten the mood and create a more positive tone in your writing. However, be mindful of the type of humor you use and ensure that it is appropriate and respectful.

Ugly words and language tags detract from the overall tone and effectiveness of your writing. By using more positive and uplifting language, you can create a more engaging and inspiring tone that will resonate with your readers.

Don't Stop Editing

Writing is a craft that requires skill, patience, and attention to detail. As a writer, you may spend countless hours working on a piece of writing, carefully crafting each sentence and paragraph to convey your message in the most effective way possible. However, the work doesn't end there. Once you have written your first draft, it's time to start the editing process. And this is where the real magic happens. Editing is what turns a good piece of writing into a great one. In this article, we'll explore why writers should never stop editing and how to approach the editing process.

Editing is an essential part of the writing process. It's the time when you go back over your work with a fine-tooth comb, checking for errors, tightening up your language, and making sure that your message is clear and concise. While editing may seem tedious and time-consuming, it's an essential step in producing high-quality writing.

One of the biggest mistakes that writers can make is thinking that their first draft is perfect. While it may be tempting to rush through the writing process and move on to the next project, taking the time to edit your work can make a world of difference. By carefully reviewing your work, you can catch errors, fix awkward sentences, and make sure that your writing is polished and professional.

Another benefit of editing is that it allows you to refine your message. As you review your work, you may find that there are areas where your message is unclear or where you need to provide more information. By taking the time to edit your work, you can make sure that your message is clear and that your readers will understand exactly what you're trying to say.

Editing is also a chance to experiment with different writing styles and techniques. As you review your work, you may find that certain sentences or paragraphs could be improved by using a different word or phrase. By playing around with your language and experimenting with different styles, you can create writing that is unique and engaging.

One of the keys to successful editing is taking a break from your work before you start the editing process. This allows you to approach your work with fresh eyes, making it easier to spot errors and identify areas that need improvement. When you come back to your work after a break, you'll be able to see your writing from a different perspective, which can be incredibly helpful when it comes to editing.

Another important aspect of editing is seeking feedback from others. While it can be difficult to hear criticism of your work, getting feedback from others can be incredibly helpful in identifying areas where you may need to improve. Whether it's from a trusted friend, colleague, or writing group, feedback can help you see your work from a different perspective and make the necessary changes to improve your writing.

Editing is an essential part of the writing process. By taking the time to carefully review your work, you can catch errors, refine your message, experiment with different styles, and create writing that is polished and professional. While editing may be time-consuming, it's a necessary step in producing high-quality writing. With a little time and effort, you can turn a good piece of writing into a great one.

Don't Stop Proofreading

As a writer, you know how important it is to create work that is polished and professional. You've spent hours crafting your sentences and paragraphs, carefully choosing your words, and organizing your ideas. But your work is not done yet. Once you have finished writing, it's time to start proofreading.

Proofreading is an essential step in the writing process. It's the time when you go back over your work with a fine-tooth comb, checking for errors, typos, and other mistakes. While it may seem tedious and time-consuming, proofreading is an essential step in producing high-quality writing.

One of the biggest mistakes that writers can make is thinking that their work is error-free. No matter how skilled you are, everyone makes mistakes. Typos, grammatical errors, and other mistakes can sneak into your writing, even if you're an experienced writer. That's why proofreading is so important. By carefully reviewing your work, you can catch errors that you may have missed the first time around.

When proofreading your work, it's important to take your time. Don't rush through your writing and assume that everything is correct. Instead, take the time to read each sentence carefully, looking for mistakes and errors. You may even want to read your work out loud, as this can help you catch errors that you may have missed while reading silently.

Another important aspect of proofreading is using tools to help you. There are many online tools and software programs available that can help you catch errors in your writing. These tools can check your grammar, spelling, and punctuation, making it easier for you to catch mistakes and improve your writing. If Microsoft Word is underlining a word in red, check it out!

While proofreading your own work is important, it's also a good idea (depending on the size of your project) to hire a professional proofreader. A professional proofreader can help you catch errors that you may have missed, as well as provide feedback on your writing. A proofreader can also help you ensure that your work is polished and professional, making it more likely to be accepted by publishers and readers.

When hiring a proofreader, it's important to choose someone who is experienced and knowledgeable. Look for a proofreader who has worked with other writers in your genre, as this can help ensure that they understand the unique needs of your work. You may also want to ask for references and read reviews from other writers to ensure that you are working with someone who is reliable and trustworthy.

Proofreading is an essential step in the writing process. By carefully reviewing your work and using tools to help you, you can catch errors and improve the quality of your writing. And if you want to ensure that your work is polished and professional, consider hiring a professional proofreader. With their expertise and experience, a proofreader can help you catch errors and refine your writing, making it more likely to be successful.

Multitasking Can Increase Productivity

Have you ever found yourself feeling stuck on a particular writing project, unable to come up with new ideas or find the right words? If so, you're not alone. Many writers experience periods of creative block, when their minds feel empty and uninspired. One effective strategy for overcoming this block is to work on more than one writing project at a time.

When you work on multiple writing projects simultaneously, you give yourself the opportunity to shift your focus and energy between different tasks. This can help you stay motivated and engaged, as well as prevent burnout and mental fatigue. In addition, working on multiple projects can help you develop your writing skills and explore different genres, styles, and topics.

One of the benefits of working on multiple projects is that it can help you avoid getting too attached to any one idea. Sometimes writers become so invested in a particular project that they struggle to see it objectively. They may become bogged down in details or struggle to find new angles or perspectives. By working on multiple projects, you give yourself the opportunity to step back and gain fresh insight, which can help you see your work in a new light.

Another benefit of working on multiple projects is that it can help you build a diverse writing portfolio. If you're a writer who is interested in pursuing a career in writing, having a variety of writing samples can be beneficial when you're looking for work or trying to get published. By working on multiple projects, you can showcase your range and versatility as a writer, which can help you stand out from the competition.

When you're working on multiple projects, it's important to stay organized and manage your time effectively. One way to do this is to create a schedule or to-do list that outlines your goals and deadlines for each project. This can help you stay focused and ensure that you're making progress on all of your writing projects.

It's also important to be realistic about how much time and energy you can dedicate to each project. Make sure that you're not overextending yourself or taking on too much work at once. Remember that quality is more important than quantity, and that it's better to produce a few well-written pieces than a lot of mediocre ones.

In addition to managing your time effectively, it's also important to take care of yourself and prioritize self-care. Working on multiple projects can be mentally and emotionally taxing, and it's important to give yourself time to rest and recharge. This might mean taking breaks throughout the day, getting enough sleep, or engaging in other activities that help you feel relaxed and refreshed. Personally, I use yoga because it requires me to focus on myself, and not on whatever project I'm struggling with.

Working on multiple writing projects can be a valuable strategy for writers who want to improve their skills, stay motivated, and explore new ideas and genres. By managing your time effectively, staying organized, and prioritizing self-care, you can successfully juggle multiple writing projects and achieve your writing goals. So if you're feeling stuck or uninspired on a particular project, consider taking on a new challenge by working on multiple projects at once. You might be surprised at the results!

Vary Sentence Length to Create Rhythm

When it comes to writing, there are few things more important than mastering sentence structure. Sentence structure is the backbone of any written work, and it can make or break the flow of your story or essay. One of the key elements of sentence structure is sentence length. By varying the length of your sentences, you can create rhythm and flow in your writing.

Rhythm is an important aspect of writing, and it can be achieved by varying the length of your sentences. Short sentences can create a staccato rhythm, which can be used to create a sense of urgency or tension in your writing. Long sentences, on the other hand, can create a more languid and relaxed rhythm, which can be used to create a sense of calm or contemplation. Mixing short and long sentences can create a varied rhythm that keeps your writing interesting and engaging.

Varying the length of your sentences also helps to avoid monotony in your writing. If you use the same sentence length repeatedly, your writing can become dull and tedious to read. This is why it's important to mix it up and use a variety of sentence lengths.

Using short sentences can also be an effective way to emphasize a point or create emphasis. Short sentences are often used for impact, and can be a great way to make a point stand out. They can also be used to break up longer, more complex sentences, making your writing easier to read and understand.

Long sentences, on the other hand, can be used to convey complex ideas or detailed descriptions. They can help to slow the pace of your writing and allow your reader to fully immerse themselves in the story or description. However, it's important to use long sentences in moderation, as they can be overwhelming if used too frequently.

Another way to vary the length of your sentences is to use sentence fragments. Sentence fragments are incomplete sentences, and they can be used to create a sense of immediacy or urgency in your writing. They can also be used to add emphasis to a point or idea.

It's important to note, however, that sentence fragments should be used sparingly. Too many sentence fragments can make your writing choppy and difficult to read, and can ultimately detract from your message.

When it comes to sentence length, there are a few guidelines to keep in mind. First, make sure to mix it up and use a variety of sentence lengths. This will help to keep your writing interesting and engaging. Second, use short sentences for impact and long sentences for detail. Finally, don't be afraid to use sentence fragments to add emphasis or urgency to your writing, but use them in moderation.

By mixing up your sentence length and using short and long sentences in moderation, you can create writing that is interesting, engaging, and easy to read. When writing, always keep sentence

length in mind and experiment with different sentence structures
to create a dynamic and compelling piece of writing.

Add Variety with Different Sentence Structures

Writing is an art form, and like any art form, it's important to add variety to keep the reader engaged. One way to do this is by using different sentence structures. Writing in the same sentence structure throughout the piece can become monotonous and boring. However, using different sentence structures can help to add depth, variety, and interest to your writing.

Here are some tips on how to vary your sentence structures:

▸ **Use simple sentences:** Simple sentences contain a subject and a verb and express a complete thought. They are often short and to the point, making them easy to read and understand.

▸ **Use compound sentences:** Compound sentences contain two or more independent clauses joined by a conjunction such as "and," "but," or "or." They allow you to connect ideas and show the relationship between them.

▸ **Use complex sentences**: Complex sentences contain one independent clause and one or more dependent clauses. They allow you to express more complicated ideas and show the relationship between different parts of a sentence.

‣ **Use parallel structure:** Parallel structure means that the structure of each sentence is the same. For example, "She likes to read, swim, and hike." This creates a rhythm and makes the sentence easier to read.

‣ **Use varied sentence lengths:** Varying sentence lengths can create a sense of rhythm and help to add interest to your writing. Short sentences can create a sense of urgency or excitement, while longer sentences can be used to provide more detail or explanation.

‣ **Use rhetorical questions:** Rhetorical questions are questions that are not meant to be answered, but instead, are used to create a sense of drama or tension. They can also be used to emphasize a point or to encourage the reader to think about something in a different way.

‣ **Use passive voice:** While it's generally advised to use active voice, using passive voice can be effective in certain situations. Passive voice is when the subject of the sentence is acted upon, rather than performing the action. For example, "The book was read by her." This can create a sense of detachment or distance from the subject.

‣ **Use inverted sentences:** Inverted sentences are sentences where the verb comes before the subject. For example, "In the garden, the flowers bloomed." This can be used to create emphasis and draw attention to a particular part of the sentence.

By using different sentence structures, you can add variety and interest to your writing. However, it's important to remember that variety should not come at the expense of clarity. Always make sure that your writing is easy to read and understand, and that the structure of your sentences supports your message.

Avoid Run-On Sentences and Fragments

Writing is a powerful tool that allows us to communicate our thoughts and ideas to others. However, not all writing is created equal. Some writing can be confusing and difficult to read, while others are clear and easy to understand. As a writer, it's important to be mindful of the structure and flow of your writing, as it can have a significant impact on the readability and effectiveness of your message. In this article, we will explore why writers should avoid run-on sentences and sentence fragments, and provide tips on how to improve the structure and flow of your writing.

First and foremost, it's important to define what we mean by run-on sentences and sentence fragments. A run-on sentence is a sentence that goes on for too long and is often difficult to read or understand. Run-on sentences can occur when a writer tries to include too many ideas or thoughts in one sentence, or when they don't use proper punctuation to separate ideas. A sentence fragment, on the other hand, is an incomplete sentence that doesn't express a complete thought or idea. Sentence fragments can occur when a writer tries to create a dramatic effect by breaking up their sentences or when they don't use proper punctuation.

One reason why writers should avoid run-on sentences and sentence fragments is that they can be difficult for readers to understand. Long sentences that go on for too long can be confusing and make it hard for readers to follow the writer's train of thought. Similarly, sentence fragments can leave readers wondering what the writer is trying to say or what point they are trying to make.

Another reason to avoid run-on sentences and sentence fragments is that they can detract from the overall tone and effectiveness of your writing. By using clear and concise sentences, you can create a more positive and engaging tone that will resonate with your readers.

How can writers improve the structure and flow of their writing?

- **Use punctuation correctly:** Use proper punctuation to separate ideas and create clear, concise sentences. Use commas to separate ideas within a sentence, and use periods to end a sentence and start a new one.

- **Keep sentences short:** Try to keep your sentences short and to the point. Long, complex sentences can be confusing and difficult to read, while short, concise sentences are easy to understand and can make your writing more engaging.

- **Use conjunctions:** Use conjunctions like "and," "but," and "or" to connect ideas and create more complex sentences. This can help to create a natural flow and prevent your writing from becoming too choppy or disjointed.

- **Use complete sentences:** Make sure that each sentence expresses a complete thought or idea. Sentence fragments can be confusing and leave readers wondering what you're trying to say.

▸ **Read your writing out loud:** Reading your writing out loud can help you identify run-on sentences and sentence fragments. It can also help you identify areas where your writing may be unclear or difficult to understand.

In conclusion, writers should avoid run-on sentences and sentence fragments in their writing, as they can be difficult to read, detract from the effectiveness of your message, and make your writing less engaging. By using proper punctuation, keeping your sentences short, using conjunctions, using complete sentences, and reading your writing out loud, you can improve the structure and flow of your writing and create a more engaging and effective message that will resonate with your readers. So, the next time you sit down to write, remember to be mindful of the structure and flow of your writing, and focus on creating clear, concise sentences that are easy to understand and engaging to read.

Use Transitions to Make Your Writing Flow

As a writer, one of your most important jobs is to help your reader move smoothly from one idea to the next. When your ideas are disconnected or your writing lacks a clear path, your reader can become confused or lost. That's where transitions come in.

Transitions are words or phrases that help connect one idea to the next, making your writing flow more smoothly. They can be simple, like "first," "second," and "finally," or more complex, like "despite," "in contrast to," and "furthermore." By using transitions effectively, you can guide your reader through your ideas and make your writing more enjoyable to read.

Here's how to use transitions effectively:

▸ Use transitions to show the relationship between ideas: Transitions can help you show how one idea relates to another. For example, if you're writing about the benefits of exercise, you might use the transition "furthermore" to show that you're adding another point to support your argument.

Or you might use the transition "however" to show that you're introducing a contrasting idea.

▸ Use transitions to show the passage of time: Transitions can also help you show the passage of time. For example, if you're writing a narrative essay, you might use the transition "later" to show that time has passed and you're moving on to a new event. Or you might use the transition "meanwhile" to show that two events are happening at the same time.

▸ Use transitions to add emphasis: Transitions can also be used to add emphasis to your writing. For example, if you're making a particularly important point, you might use the transition "indeed" to show that you really mean what you're saying. Or you might use the transition "above all" to show that something is the most important thing to consider.

▸ Use transitions sparingly: While transitions can be helpful, it's important not to overuse them. Too many transitions can make your writing seem choppy or forced. Use transitions only when they're necessary to connect your ideas or make your writing flow more smoothly.

▸ Vary your transitions: Using the same transitions over and over again can also make your writing seem repetitive. Try to vary your transitions by using different words or phrases to show the relationship between your ideas.

▸ Practice using transitions: Like any writing skill, using transitions effectively takes practice. As you write, pay attention to how you're connecting your ideas and think about how you could use transitions to make your writing flow more smoothly. You might also try reading other writers and paying attention to how they use transitions in their work.

Using transitions is a simple yet powerful way to make your writing more enjoyable to read. By helping your reader move smoothly from one idea to the next, you can create a clear and compelling argument or narrative that leaves a lasting impression

Make 'Em Laugh

Writing is a form of art that allows us to communicate our thoughts and feelings to others. One of the most effective ways to engage your reader and make your writing more enjoyable is by using humor. Humor can help you connect with your readers, make them laugh, and even convey complex ideas in a lighthearted way.

One way to incorporate humor into your writing is by using satire. Satire is a form of humor that uses irony, sarcasm, and ridicule to expose and criticize human folly and vices. It can be a powerful tool for commenting on social issues or pointing out flaws in a particular system or institution. However, it is important to be careful when using satire, as it can be easily misunderstood or taken out of context.

Another way to use humor in your writing is by incorporating witty one-liners or puns. These can be effective for adding a touch of humor to an otherwise serious piece of writing. However, it is important to not overdo it, as too many jokes or puns can become tiresome and take away from the overall message of your writing.

A third way to use humor in your writing is by using self-deprecating humor. This is when you make fun of yourself or your own experiences in a lighthearted way. Self-deprecating humor can help to humanize you and make you more relatable to your readers. It can also help to diffuse any tension or anxiety your readers may feel about the subject matter.

One important thing to remember when using humor in your writing is to be authentic. Don't force humor into your writing if it doesn't come naturally to you. If you are naturally a serious person, then it may be difficult for you to use humor effectively in your writing. However, if you have a natural talent for making people laugh, then don't be afraid to use it to your advantage.

Using humor in your writing can be a very effective way to engage your readers and make your writing more enjoyable. However, it is important to understand your audience, make sure that your humor is relevant to the topic at hand, and use humor in moderation. Whether you use satire, one-liners, or self-deprecating humor, the key is to be authentic and let your natural humor shine through in your writing.

Use Analogies to Explain Complex Ideas

It can be challenging to communicate complex ideas to your readers in a way that they can easily understand. This is where analogies come in. An analogy is a comparison between two things, typically to explain or clarify a concept. Analogies can be an incredibly powerful tool in your writing arsenal, as they help to break down complex ideas and make them more accessible to your readers.

Analogies work by taking something familiar to your readers and using it to explain something unfamiliar. For example, if you were trying to explain the concept of the internet to someone who had never used it before, you might use the analogy of a library. Just as a library is a vast collection of books and information that you can access, the internet is a vast collection of websites and information that you can access.

Analogies can be used in a variety of ways in your writing. They can be used to explain scientific concepts, technical jargon, or abstract ideas. They can also be used to add depth and meaning to your writing, or to make your writing more engaging and memorable.

One of the main benefits of using analogies in your writing is that they help to make your writing more relatable to your readers. By using analogies, you can connect with your readers on a deeper level, as you are using language that they are familiar with. This helps to build trust and credibility with your readers, as they feel that you are speaking their language.

Analogies can also be used to simplify complex ideas. By breaking down complex ideas into simpler terms, you can make your writing more accessible to a wider audience. This is particularly important if you are writing for a non-specialist audience, as you need to ensure that your writing is easy to understand.

Another benefit of using analogies in your writing is that they can be used to add humor and personality to your writing. Analogies are often used in jokes and puns, and by using them in your writing, you can make your writing more engaging and entertaining. This can be particularly useful if you are writing for a younger audience, as they are often more receptive to humor and wit.

When using analogies in your writing, it is important to choose your analogies carefully. You want to make sure that the analogy you use is appropriate for your audience and purpose. You also want to make sure that your analogy is accurate and relevant to the concept you are trying to explain.

One way to ensure that your analogies are effective is to test them out on a small group of people before using them in your writing. This can help you to gauge whether your analogy is working or not, and can also help you to refine and improve your analogy if necessary.

Used properly, analogies can be an incredibly powerful tool in your writing arsenal. They can be used to explain complex ideas, simplify technical jargon, and add humor and personality to your writing.

Repetition, Repetition, Repetition

You have the power to create an impact with your words. One way to do this is through the effective use of repetition. Repetition is the act of repeating a word or phrase for emphasis or effect. It can be a powerful tool for writers because it helps to reinforce an idea and create a sense of rhythm and familiarity in your writing.

There are several ways that repetition can be used in writing. One of the most common is to repeat a key phrase or word throughout a piece of writing. This can be done for emphasis or to create a memorable effect. For example, in Martin Luther King Jr.'s famous "I Have a Dream" speech, he repeats the phrase "I have a dream" several times to emphasize his vision of a more equal and just society.

Repetition can also be used to create a sense of rhythm and flow in your writing. By repeating certain words or phrases, you can create a pattern that draws the reader in and keeps them engaged. This can be particularly effective in poetry and song lyrics, where repetition is often used to create a specific meter or rhyme scheme.

Another way to use repetition in writing is to repeat a theme or idea throughout a piece of writing. This can help to reinforce the central message of your writing and create a cohesive structure. For example, if you're writing a story about overcoming adversity, you could repeat the theme of resilience throughout the story to reinforce the message of perseverance.

Repetition can also be used to create a sense of urgency or intensity in your writing. By repeating certain words or phrases, you can create a sense of urgency and make your writing more compelling. This is often used in advertising and marketing to create a sense of urgency around a product or service.

However, it's important to use repetition carefully and purposefully. Overuse of repetition can be tedious and irritating for readers. It's important to vary your word choice and sentence structure to keep your writing fresh and interesting. Additionally, repetition should be used in moderation and only when it serves a specific purpose in your writing.

Use Alliteration to Add Emphasis

If you want to add some oomph to your writing, you might consider using alliteration. Alliteration is the repetition of initial consonant sounds in a series of words within a sentence or phrase. For example, "Peter Piper picked a peck of pickled peppers" is a famous alliterative phrase.

Using alliteration can help your writing to flow smoothly, creating a pleasing sound that can engage and entertain your readers. By repeating consonant sounds, alliteration can also draw attention to certain words or ideas, emphasizing their importance and making them more memorable.

Alliteration can be used in various ways. One way is to use it to create a sense of rhythm or musicality in your writing. This can help to make your words more memorable and enjoyable to read. For example, consider the sentence "Sally sells seashells by the seashore." The repetition of the "s" sound creates a sense of rhythm and musicality that makes the sentence memorable.

Another way to use alliteration is to emphasize specific words or ideas. For example, you might write "The shimmering sun slowly sank into the sea," emphasizing the sun's beauty and movement by repeating the "s" sound. Alternatively, you might write "The cat crept cautiously closer," emphasizing the cat's careful movement by repeating the "c" sound.

Alliteration can also be used to create a sense of humor or playfulness in your writing. For example, you might write "Polly put the kettle on, Peter picked a peck of pickled peppers" to create a whimsical and playful tone.

However, it's important to use alliteration sparingly and purposefully. If overused, it can come off as gimmicky and perhaps annoying. Additionally, not all writing is well-suited to alliteration.

Alliteration can be a useful tool in your writing arsenal, adding rhythm, emphasis, and playfulness to your words. Just be sure to use it purposefully and appropriately.

Use Onomatopoeia to Add Sound

As a writer, one of your goals is to make your writing come alive for your readers. One way to do this is by using onomatopoeia. Onomatopoeia is a literary device where a word sounds like the thing it is describing. It is often used to create a vivid sensory experience for the reader. Using onomatopoeia can add a layer of depth to your writing, making it more engaging and memorable.

When you use onomatopoeia in your writing, you are essentially giving your readers a sound effect to accompany the action in your story. For example, if you're writing a story about a thunderstorm, you might use words like "rumble" or "crash" to describe the sound of thunder. By doing so, you create a more immersive experience for your reader, allowing them to visualize the scene in their mind's eye.

Onomatopoeia can be used in a variety of different contexts, from poetry to prose to advertising. In poetry, onomatopoeia is often used to create a specific rhythm or to enhance the musicality of the poem. In the poem "The Bells" by Edgar Allan Poe, he uses onomatopoeic words like "tinkle" and "clang" to create a musical effect that mimics the sound of bells.

In advertising, onomatopoeia is often used to create a memorable tagline or slogan. Think of slogans like "Snap, Crackle, Pop" for Rice Krispies or "Melts in Your Mouth, Not in Your Hand" for M&M's. These slogans use onomatopoeia to create a catchy and memorable phrase that sticks in the mind of the consumer.

Using onomatopoeia in your writing can also be a useful tool for creating tone and mood. For example, if you're writing a horror story, you might use words like "creak" or "groan" to describe the sounds of a haunted house. These words create a sense of tension and unease, adding to the overall mood of the story.

Onomatopoeia should be used sparingly and appropriately. Overusing onomatopoeia can make your writing feel gimmicky or childish. It's important to choose your words carefully and only use onomatopoeia when it adds value to your writing.

By using words that sound like the things they describe, you can create a more immersive experience for your reader, making your writing more engaging and memorable.

Use Hyperbole to Add Drama

Hyperbole is a literary device that is often used in writing to add drama and emphasis to a message. It is a technique that uses exaggerated statements or claims that are not meant to be taken literally. By using hyperbole, writers can make their writing more engaging and memorable for their readers.

First and foremost, it's important to understand what hyperbole is and how it works. Hyperbole is an exaggeration used to emphasize a point or create a dramatic effect. It is a tool that writers can use to grab their reader's attention and make their writing more interesting. Hyperbole is often used in creative writing, poetry, and speeches to add drama and emotion to the message.

One way to use hyperbole is to exaggerate the importance or impact of a particular event or situation. For example, you could write, "The storm was so powerful that it shook the earth and brought trees crashing down around us." This statement exaggerates the intensity of the storm, making it more dramatic and memorable for the reader.

Another way to use hyperbole is to exaggerate the characteristics of a person or object. For example, you could write,

"Her eyes were as big as saucers and shone like diamonds in the sun." This statement exaggerates the size and sparkle of the woman's eyes, creating a vivid image in the reader's mind.

Everyone can use a little hyperbole in their work! Here's some pointers:

▸ **Use hyperbole sparingly:** Hyperbole should be used sparingly to avoid overwhelming the reader and detracting from the message you are trying to convey. Too much hyperbole can make your writing seem exaggerated and unbelievable.

▸ **Use hyperbole to create an emotional response:** Hyperbole is most effective when used to create an emotional response in the reader. Use hyperbole to emphasize the impact of a particular event or situation, or to create an image that will stay with the reader long after they have finished reading.

▸ **Use hyperbole to emphasize a point:** Hyperbole can be an effective tool for emphasizing a particular point or argument. Use hyperbole to draw attention to the importance of a particular issue or to create a sense of urgency in the reader.

▸ **Use hyperbole to create humor:** Hyperbole can also be used to create humor in your writing. Use hyperbole to exaggerate a particular characteristic or situation in a way that is funny or absurd.

▸ **Use hyperbole to create vivid imagery:** Hyperbole can be an effective tool for creating vivid imagery in your writing. Use hyperbole to describe a person or object in a way that will create a clear image in the reader's mind.

Using hyperbole the right way you just might write the single most incredible book in the history of the human race. (Yes, you're correct ... that's hyperbole).

Use Irony to Make a Point

Irony is a literary device that can be used to add humor or make a point in writing. It is a tool that allows writers to convey a message in a way that is unexpected or contradictory to what the reader might expect.

Irony is often used in writing to create a humorous effect, but it can also be used to make a serious point. There are several types of irony, including verbal irony, situational irony, and dramatic irony. Verbal irony is when a person says one thing but means the opposite. Situational irony occurs when there is a discrepancy between what is expected to happen and what actually happens. Dramatic irony is when the reader knows something that the characters in the story do not.

One way to use irony in writing is to create a humorous effect. This can be done by using verbal irony to create a statement that is unexpected or contradictory. For example, you could write, "It was a beautiful day for a picnic, except for the rain." This statement is ironic because a beautiful day is not typically associated with rain, and it creates a humorous effect.

Irony can also be used to make a serious point. This can be done by using situational irony to highlight a discrepancy between what is expected to happen and what actually happens. For example, you could write about a politician who is known for his honesty, but is caught lying. This situation is ironic because it is unexpected, and it highlights the discrepancy between the politician's reputation and his actions.

Here's a few tips for using irony effectively:

▸ **Use irony sparingly:** Irony should be used sparingly to avoid overwhelming the reader and detracting from the message you are trying to convey. Too much irony can make your writing seem contrived and unbelievable.

▸ **Use irony to create a contrast:** Irony is most effective when used to create a contrast between what is expected and what actually happens. Use irony to highlight a discrepancy or to create a surprising twist.

▸ **Use irony to make a point:** Irony can be an effective tool for making a point in your writing. Use irony to highlight a problem or to bring attention to an issue.

▸ **Use irony to create humor:** Irony can also be used to create humor in your writing. Use irony to create a statement that is unexpected or contradictory in a way that is humorous or absurd.

▸ **Use irony to create suspense:** Irony can be an effective tool for creating suspense in your writing. Use dramatic irony to create a situation where the reader knows something that the characters in the story do not.

When using irony in your writing, it's important to be mindful of its impact on the message you are trying to convey. While irony can be an effective tool for adding humor or making a point, it can also detract from the credibility of your writing if it is overused or not used appropriately.

Satire: Use with Caution

Satire is a powerful tool that writers use to criticize or make fun of a subject. It's a form of humor that can be used to bring attention to important issues or to make a point.

Satire is a type of humor that uses irony, sarcasm, and exaggeration to criticize or poke fun at a subject. It's often used to bring attention to social or political issues and to challenge the status quo.

One way to use satire in writing is to directly criticize a subject. This can be done by using satire to highlight the flaws or shortcomings of a person, organization, or institution. Satire can be a powerful tool for exposing the truth about a subject and bringing attention to important issues. For example, a writer might use satire to criticize a political leader who is known for making contradictory statements. By using satire to point out the leader's flaws, the writer can bring attention to the issue and encourage people to question the leader's credibility.

Another way to use satire in writing is to make fun of a subject. This can be done by using satire to create a humorous effect that pokes fun at the absurdity of a situation. Satire can be used to make people laugh while also making a point. For example, a writer might use satire to make fun of a popular trend or fad that has become ridiculous. By using satire to create a humorous effect, the writer can bring attention to the issue and encourage people to think critically about it.

Here are some tips for using satire effectively:

▸ **Know your audience:** Satire can be a powerful tool for engaging your audience, but it's important to know your audience before using it. Satire can be misinterpreted or misunderstood by some people, so it's important to use it only with an audience that will appreciate and understand it.

▸ **Be clear about your message:** Satire can be a powerful tool for making a point, but it's important to be clear about your message. Make sure your satire is focused and clear so that your audience understands the point you are trying to make.

▸ **Use irony and exaggeration:** Satire is most effective when it uses irony and exaggeration to highlight the flaws or absurdity of a subject. Use these techniques to create a humorous effect that will engage your audience and make them think.

▸ **Avoid being offensive:** Satire can be a powerful tool for making a point, but it's important to avoid being offensive. Satire should be used to criticize or make fun of a subject, not to attack or belittle individuals or groups.

▸ **Use satire to inspire change:** Satire can be an effective tool for inspiring change. Use your satire to bring attention to important issues and to encourage people to take action.

When using satire in your writing, it's important to be mindful of the impact it can have on your message. While satire can be an effective tool for criticizing or making fun of a subject, it can also be misinterpreted or misunderstood. Use it with caution.

Poke Fun with Parody

Parody is a form of humor that writers use to imitate a well-known work or style for humorous effect. It's a way of poking fun at something in a lighthearted way that can bring joy and entertainment to readers.

One way to use parody in writing is to imitate a well-known work or style. This can be done by using parody to create a humorous effect that pokes fun at the original work or style. Parody can be a powerful tool for creating entertainment while also making a point. For example, a writer might use parody to create a humorous effect that imitates a famous novel or movie. By using parody to poke fun at the original work, the writer can create an entertaining piece that also makes a commentary on the original work or style.

Another way to use parody in writing is to create a humorous effect that mocks a person, organization, or institution. This can be done by using parody to imitate the mannerisms, behaviors, or beliefs of the person or organization being mocked. Parody can be used to create a humorous effect that makes people laugh while also highlighting the absurdity of the subject being mocked. For example, a writer might use parody to create a humorous effect that imitates a famous politician's speeches. By using parody to mock the politician's mannerisms, the writer can create a humorous piece that also points out the flaws in the politician's style and message.

When using parody in your writing, it's important to be mindful of the impact it can have on your message. While it can be an effective tool for creating entertainment and making a point, it can also be misinterpreted or misunderstood.

Here are some tips for using parody effectively:

▸ **Know your audience:** Parody can be a powerful tool for engaging your audience, but it's important to know your audience before using it. Parody can be misinterpreted or misunderstood by some people, so it's important to use it only with an audience that will appreciate and understand it.

▸ **Be clear about your message:** Parody can be a powerful tool for making a point, but it's important to be clear about your message. Make sure your parody is focused and clear so that your audience understands the point you are trying to make.

▸ **Use humor and exaggeration:** Parody is most effective when it uses humor and exaggeration to highlight the flaws or absurdity of a subject. Use these techniques to create a humorous effect that will engage your audience and make them think.

▸ **Avoid being offensive:** Parody should be used to create entertainment and humor, not to attack or belittle individuals or groups. Avoid using parody in a way that could be seen as offensive or hurtful.

▸ **Use parody to inspire change:** Parody can be an effective tool for inspiring change. Use your parody to bring attention to important issues and to encourage people to take action.

Parody is a powerful tool that writers can use to imitate a well-known work or style for humorous effect. By knowing your audience, being clear about your message, using humor and exaggeration, avoiding being offensive, and using parody to inspire change, you can use parody effectively in your writing to engage and entertain your readers.

Make Your Characters Authentic with Jargon

Jargon is a specialized language that is used by individuals within a particular profession, industry, or group. It is often associated with technical or specialized terms that are not commonly used in everyday language. When used effectively, jargon can add authenticity to your characters and make them seem more realistic.

Using jargon in your writing can be a powerful tool for creating more authentic characters. Jargon is often used by individuals within a particular profession or industry and is specific to that group. By using this specialized slang in your writing, you can create characters who are more believable and realistic.

When using jargon in your writing, it's important to understand the context in which it is used. This type of language is often used in specific situations or contexts, and it's important to use it correctly in order to avoid sounding forced or artificial. For example, if you're writing a story about a group of doctors, you would want to use medical jargon to make the characters seem more authentic. However, if you use medical terminology in a scene where the doctors are having a casual conversation outside of work, it might seem out of place and forced.

Using jargon effectively in your writing requires a good understanding of the profession or industry you are writing about. It's important to research the specific jargon used in that field and to use it correctly. Using jargon incorrectly can make your characters seem less authentic and can distract your readers from the story.

Jargon can also be used to create a sense of insider knowledge or expertise. By using an insider's specialized language, you can create characters who are experts in their field and who are able to communicate effectively with others in their profession or industry. This can add depth to your characters and make them more interesting to readers.

However, it's important to use jargon in moderation. Overusing medical, legal or technical terms can make your writing difficult to read and can be off-putting to readers who are not familiar with the specific terminology. It's important to strike a balance between using enough jargon to create authentic characters and not using so much that it becomes overwhelming.

By understanding the context in which it is used, researching the specific jargon used in the profession or industry you are writing about, and using it in moderation, you can create characters who are more believable and interesting.

Metaphors and Similes Add Depth

Metaphors and similes are powerful tools for writers to create vivid and imaginative writing. They allow writers to add depth and complexity to their work by drawing comparisons between two seemingly unrelated objects or ideas. Metaphors and similes can help to create visual imagery and make abstract concepts more concrete, allowing readers to fully immerse themselves in the story or topic.

So, how can you use metaphors and similes effectively in your writing?

▸ **Use them sparingly:** While metaphors and similes can add depth to your writing, it's important to use them sparingly. Overuse can lead to cluttered writing, making it difficult for readers to understand your intended message. Use them only when necessary and make sure they are relevant to the topic at hand.

▸ **Avoid clichés:** Clichéd metaphors and similes can make your writing seem unoriginal and lazy. For example, "as light as a feather" or "as busy as a bee." Instead, try to come up with fresh, original comparisons that will surprise and delight your readers.

▸ **Be specific:** Specificity is key when it comes to creating effective metaphors and similes. Rather than relying on broad, general comparisons, try to find specific details that will make your writing stand out. For example, instead of saying "she was as cold as ice," you could say "her words were like icicles, sharp and cutting."

▸ **Use them to evoke emotion:** Metaphors and similes can be a powerful way to evoke emotion in your readers. By choosing comparisons that resonate with your readers' experiences or feelings, you can create a more emotional connection with your audience. For example, "her heart was a tangled knot of anxiety" or "his smile was like a warm embrace."

▸ **Experiment with different types of metaphors and similes:** There are many different types of metaphors and similes that you can use to add depth and complexity to your writing. Some examples include extended metaphors, where a comparison is developed over the course of several sentences or even paragraphs, and mixed metaphors, where two or more metaphors are combined to create a unique comparison. Experiment with different types of metaphors and similes to find what works best for your writing style.

Avoid Cliches and Overused Phrases

As a writer, it can be tempting to use cliches and overused phrases in your writing. After all, they are familiar, comfortable, and easy to remember. However, using cliches and overused phrases can make your writing seem unoriginal, lazy, and even boring. To make your writing stand out, it's important to avoid these common traps and come up with fresh, original language that will surprise and delight your readers.

Please, try to avoid cliches and overused phrases in your writing! Here are some tips to help you get started:

> **Identify common phrases and cliches:** The first step to avoiding cliches and overused phrases is to identify them. Take some time to go through your writing and look for any phrases that you've heard or read many times before. These might include phrases like "at the end of the day" or "in the nick of time." Once you've identified these phrases, try to come up with fresh, original alternatives.

> **Use specific, descriptive language:** One way to avoid cliches and overused phrases is to use specific, descriptive language. Instead of relying on broad, general terms, try to

find specific details that will make your writing stand out. For example, instead of saying "the sky was beautiful," you could say "the sky was a riot of colors, with streaks of pink, orange, and gold."

▸ **Use metaphors and similes:** Metaphors and similes are powerful tools for writers to add depth and complexity to their work. By drawing comparisons between two seemingly unrelated objects or ideas, you can create vivid imagery and make abstract concepts more concrete. However, it's important to avoid cliched metaphors and similes, like "as busy as a bee" or "as brave as a lion." Instead, try to come up with fresh, original comparisons that will surprise and delight your readers.

▸ **Use active voice:** Using active voice in your writing can help you avoid cliches and overused phrases. Active voice is more direct and engaging than passive voice, making your writing more interesting and memorable. Instead of saying "the cake was eaten by the dog," you could say "the dog ate the cake."

▸ **Experiment with different sentence structures:** Another way to avoid cliches and overused phrases is to experiment with different sentence structures. Try to vary the length and structure of your sentences to create a more interesting and engaging rhythm. For example, you could use short, punchy sentences to create tension, or long, flowing sentences to create a sense of calm.

Avoiding cliches and overused phrases is an important part of creating original and engaging writing. By identifying common phrases and cliches, using specific and descriptive language, using metaphors and similes, using active voice, and experimenting with different sentence structures, you can create writing that is fresh, original, and memorable. So, the next time you sit down to write, challenge yourself to avoid the familiar and find new ways to express yourself.

Try Foreshadowing to Hint at Future Events

Have you ever read a book or watched a movie where something happened that completely shocked you? You might have thought, "How did I not see that coming?" Well, chances are that the author or screenwriter used foreshadowing to hint at what was to come, but you just didn't pick up on it.

Foreshadowing is a powerful tool that writers can use to add depth and complexity to their stories. It involves dropping hints or clues about what might happen later on in the story. It can be subtle or more obvious, but either way, it helps to create anticipation and suspense in the reader.

How do you use foreshadowing effectively in your writing? Here are a few tips to get you started:

- **Plan ahead:** Foreshadowing works best when it is planned in advance. You need to know where your story is going in order to drop hints about what's to come. Take some time to think about the key events in your story and how you can hint at them earlier on.

▸ **Use symbolism:** Symbolism is a great way to foreshadow events without being too obvious. For example, if you have a character who is always wearing a particular piece of jewelry, you could use that to foreshadow a key event later on in the story.

▸ **Be subtle:** Foreshadowing doesn't have to be obvious. In fact, it's often more effective when it's subtle. Use hints and clues that are easy to miss on a first read-through but become more apparent on subsequent readings.

▸ **Use dialogue:** Dialogue is a great way to foreshadow events, especially if you have a character who is particularly perceptive or intuitive. They might pick up on something that other characters miss, giving the reader a clue about what's to come.

▸ **Use descriptive language:** Descriptive language can also be used to foreshadow events. For example, if you're describing a stormy night, you could use language that hints at danger or impending doom.

▸ **Don't give too much away:** While foreshadowing is important, you don't want to give too much away. You still want your reader to be surprised and shocked when the key events happen. Use foreshadowing to create anticipation, but don't reveal too much.

▸ **Use foreshadowing throughout the story:** Foreshadowing shouldn't just be used at the beginning of the story. You can drop hints and clues throughout the story to create a sense of tension and anticipation.

Foreshadowing can be a powerful tool in your writing arsenal, but it's important to use it effectively. Don't overdo it, and make sure that you're not giving too much away. Use subtle hints and clues to create anticipation and suspense, and your readers will be on the edge of their seats until the very end.

Add Meaning with Symbolism

As a writer, you have a powerful tool at your disposal: symbolism. Symbolism is a technique in writing that uses objects, people, or situations to represent abstract ideas or themes. It's a way of creating deeper meaning in your work, and it can add a layer of complexity and richness that can make your writing more memorable and impactful.

One of the most famous examples of symbolism in literature is the green light in F. Scott Fitzgerald's The Great Gatsby. Throughout the novel, the green light that Jay Gatsby is always reaching for represents his longing for the past, and the impossibility of ever truly recapturing it. It's a powerful symbol that adds a layer of depth to the story, and it's a great example of how symbolism can be used to create meaning.

So how can you use symbolism in your own writing?

Start with your themes: Symbolism is all about representing abstract ideas or themes through concrete objects or situations. So before you can start using symbolism in your writing, you need to identify the themes you want to explore. Think about the big ideas that you want to convey in your work - love, loss, freedom, power, etc. - and then brainstorm objects, people, or situations that could represent those themes.

Use objects: One of the easiest ways to use symbolism in your writing is through objects. These can be anything from a rose to a mirror to a piece of jewelry. The key is to choose an object that has some kind of inherent meaning or association, and then use it to represent a larger idea or theme. For example, a rose might represent love or beauty, while a mirror might represent self-reflection or introspection.

Use people: Another way to use symbolism is through your characters. You can use a character to represent an idea or theme, or you can give them a trait or characteristic that symbolizes something larger. For example, a character who is always searching for something might represent the human desire for meaning or purpose, while a character who is always looking to the future might represent hope or optimism.

Use situations: Finally, you can use situations or events to create symbolism in your writing. This can be anything from a storm to a journey to a battle. The key is to choose a situation that has some kind of inherent meaning or significance, and then use it to represent a larger idea or theme. For example, a storm might represent turmoil or chaos, while a journey might represent personal growth or transformation.

When you're using symbolism in your writing, it's important to remember that subtlety is key. You don't want to beat your readers over the head with your symbolism - instead, you want it to be subtle and understated, something that they can discover on their own. Use your symbols sparingly, and make sure that they serve a purpose in the story.

Back in Time: Non-Linear Storytelling

As a fiction writer, one of your main goals is to keep your readers engaged and interested in your story. One way to achieve this is by using various storytelling techniques to add complexity and intrigue to your plot. Flashbacks and non-linear storytelling are two such techniques that can be incredibly effective in captivating your readers.

Flashbacks are a tool that allows you to take your reader back in time to show them events that occurred before the main story began. These flashbacks can be used to reveal key information about your characters or to create suspense by hinting at a significant event that occurred in the past. They can also be used to provide context or backstory that the reader needs to fully understand the current events of the story.

Non-linear storytelling is another tool that can be used to add complexity to your plot. Instead of telling the story in a linear fashion, with events unfolding chronologically, non-linear storytelling allows you to jump back and forth in time, weaving together different plot threads and creating a more intricate narrative structure. This can be especially effective if you have multiple characters or storylines that intersect in interesting ways.

Using flashbacks and non-linear storytelling can help to create a more layered and complex story, but it's important to use these techniques wisely. If used poorly, they can confuse readers and make the story feel disjointed. Here are a few tips to help you effectively use flashbacks and non-linear storytelling in your writing:

▸ Start with a clear idea of what you want to accomplish with the flashback or non-linear structure. What information are you trying to convey, and how does it add to the story?

▸ Make sure your flashbacks and non-linear structure are clearly marked and easy to follow. Use headings or chapter titles to indicate when the story is moving backward or forward in time.

▸ Use flashbacks and non-linear storytelling sparingly. Too many jumps back and forth in time can be disorienting for readers and make it difficult for them to follow the story.

▸ Be consistent with your tense and point of view. If you're jumping back and forth in time, it can be easy to accidentally switch tenses or points of view. Make sure you stay consistent throughout the story.

▸ Use flashbacks and non-linear storytelling to create suspense or to reveal key information. Don't use them just for the sake of being different or experimental.

▸ Make sure each flashback or non-linear section has a clear beginning, middle, and end. It should feel like a complete story in and of itself, even if it's only a small part of the larger narrative.

▸ Use flashbacks and non-linear storytelling to add depth to your characters. Showing events from their past can help readers understand their motivations and personality better.

By experimenting with different storytelling techniques like flashbacks and non-linear structures, you can take your fiction writing to the next level. Just remember to use these techniques wisely, and always keep your readers in mind. With practice and persistence, you can create complex, engaging stories that will keep your readers hooked from beginning to end.

Subtext Adds Depth

Writing is a powerful medium through which we can communicate our thoughts, feelings, and ideas. However, sometimes it can be challenging to convey everything we want to say in words. This is where the use of subtext and implied meaning can come in handy.

Subtext refers to the underlying message or meaning that is implied but not explicitly stated in a piece of writing. It can be conveyed through various elements such as dialogue, characterization, setting, and plot. Subtext allows writers to add depth and nuance to their writing, making it more interesting and engaging for readers.

One of the most effective ways to use subtext is through dialogue. In real life, people often don't say what they mean or mean what they say. They use subtext to communicate their true intentions, feelings, and desires. In writing, dialogue can be used in a similar way. By having characters say one thing while implying another, writers can create tension, conflict, and intrigue.

For example, consider this dialogue between two characters:
"Are you going to the party tonight?" John asked.

"I don't know, I haven't decided yet," Sarah replied.

On the surface, this seems like a simple exchange. However, if we read between the lines, we can infer that Sarah is not interested in going to the party. Perhaps she doesn't like the people who will be there or she's not in the mood to socialize. By using subtext, the writer has added depth to the scene, giving us insight into Sarah's character and motivations.

Another way to use subtext is through characterization. By showing rather than telling, writers can reveal a character's traits, beliefs, and values. For example, a character who is always punctual and organized might be someone who values order and control. On the other hand, a character who is always late and forgetful might be someone who values spontaneity and creativity. By using subtext, writers can create more complex and nuanced characters that readers can relate to and empathize with.

Setting can also be used to create subtext. By describing the environment in which a scene takes place, writers can convey mood, tone, and atmosphere. For example, a dark and stormy night might suggest danger, suspense, or foreboding. A bright and sunny day might suggest happiness, joy, or optimism. By using subtext, writers can enhance the emotional impact of their writing, making it more engaging and memorable for readers.

Plot is another element that can benefit from the use of subtext. By implying certain events or outcomes, writers can create suspense and intrigue. For example, a character who receives a mysterious letter might be afraid or curious about its contents. By using subtext, writers can build anticipation and keep readers engaged.

Seek Feedback

Writing is a solitary pursuit, but it doesn't have to be a lonely one. Seeking feedback from beta readers, writing groups, or a professional editor can be an incredibly helpful way to improve your writing, grow as a writer, and ultimately create a better finished product.

Beta readers are readers who read and provide feedback on an author's work before its published. They can be friends, family, or even strangers who are interested in reading your work and giving you constructive feedback. Beta readers can provide invaluable insights into your work, pointing out areas where your story might be unclear or where your characters might be inconsistent. They can also give you an idea of how your work will be received by your target audience, which can be helpful in making revisions or edits.

Joining a writing group is another great way to get feedback on your writing. Writing groups are communities of writers who meet regularly to share their work and provide feedback on each other's writing. Writing groups can be found online or in person, and they can be an excellent way to connect with other writers and get constructive feedback on your work. Writing groups can provide a safe and supportive environment for writers to share their work, and the feedback you receive can help you improve your writing skills.

If you're looking for more targeted feedback, a professional editor might be the way to go. Professional editors are experienced in the art of storytelling and can help you take your writing to the next level. They can help you with everything from plot structure and character development to grammar and punctuation. A professional editor can be especially helpful if you're looking to publish your work, as they can help you polish your manuscript to a professional standard.

When seeking feedback, it's important to keep an open mind and be willing to listen to constructive criticism. Feedback can be hard to hear, especially when it's critical, but it's important to remember that feedback is meant to help you improve your work, not tear it down. It's also important to be clear about what kind of feedback you're looking for. Are you looking for feedback on the overall structure of your story, or are you looking for feedback on the dialogue or characterization? Being clear about what you're looking for can help ensure that you receive feedback that's helpful and relevant.

It's also important to remember that feedback is subjective. What one reader might love, another might hate. Ultimately, it's up to you as the author to decide which feedback to take and which to leave. It's important to listen to feedback and consider it carefully, but at the end of the day, you're the one who knows your story best.

Seeking feedback from beta readers, writing groups, or a professional editor can be an incredibly helpful way to improve your writing. It can be scary to share your work with others, but the feedback you receive can help you identify areas where your writing can be improved, and ultimately create a better finished product. When seeking feedback, it's important to keep an open mind, be clear about what you're looking for, and remember that feedback is subjective. So don't be afraid to put yourself and your writing out there, and see how feedback can help you grow as a writer.

Don't Stop Believing

As a writer, it's important to have confidence in yourself and your abilities. Writing can be a challenging and often solitary pursuit, but with perseverance and determination, you can achieve your goals and realize your dreams.

One of the most important things that writers can do is to believe in themselves. This means having confidence in your abilities and trusting your instincts. When you believe in yourself, you're more likely to take risks, try new things, and push yourself to be better.

Of course, it's not always easy to maintain this level of confidence. Writing can be a difficult and emotional journey, and it's easy to become discouraged when things don't go as planned. That's why it's important to stay positive and keep trying, even when things are tough.

One way to maintain your confidence is to focus on your strengths as a writer. Take a moment to reflect on what you do well, whether it's creating vivid characters, writing compelling dialogue, or crafting beautiful descriptions. By focusing on your strengths, you can build your confidence and remind yourself of what you're capable of.

Another important aspect of writing is the willingness to take risks and try new things. This can mean experimenting with different genres, styles, or formats, or simply taking on new challenges in your writing. When you're willing to take risks, you open yourself up to new possibilities and opportunities for growth.

Of course, taking risks also means facing the possibility of failure. But it's important to remember that failure is not the end of the world. In fact, many successful writers have experienced their fair share of failures and rejections before achieving success. The key is to learn from your failures and use them as opportunities for growth and improvement.

In addition to believing in yourself and taking risks, it's also important to keep trying. Writing is a process, and success often comes through hard work and persistence. This means staying committed to your writing, even when it feels difficult or overwhelming.

Stay motivated by setting goals for yourself. Whether it's finishing a manuscript, submitting to a certain number of publications, or simply writing for a set amount of time each day, setting achievable goals can help you stay focused and motivated.

It's also important to find support and encouragement from others. Joining a writing group, attending conferences or workshops, or simply sharing your work with trusted friends or family members can help you stay inspired and motivated.

Writing is a journey that requires confidence, risk-taking, and persistence. By believing in yourself, taking risks, and keeping trying, you can achieve your goals and realize your dreams as a writer. So don't be afraid to take that first step, believe in yourself, and keep pushing forward.